The insanity plea /
345.04 DOLAN   30008000020401
Dolan, Edward F.,
          Berne PL
                                        04525

DATE DUE

D1490520

The
Insanity
Plea

THE INSANITY PLEA by
Edward F. Dolan, Jr.

FRANKLIN WATTS
New York | London | Toronto | Sydney | 1984
AN IMPACT BOOK

Photographs courtesy of
United Press International: pp. 5, 6, 10 (both),
34 (both), 47, 50, 58, 63, 72, 77, 80;
The Bettmann Archive: p. 27; Culver Pictures: p. 40.

Library of Congress Cataloging in Publication Data

Dolan, Edward F., 1924-
The insanity plea.

(An Impact book)
Bibliography: p.
Includes index.
Summary: An examination of the insanity plea,
how it developed, how it works, and the controversy
that surrounds it. Also discusses its effect on
the criminal justice system in the United States.
1. Insanity—Jurisprudence—United States—
Juvenile literature. [1. Insanity—Jurisprudence.
2. Law] I. Title.
KF9242.Z9D64   1984   345.73'04   83-21846
ISBN 0-531-04756-3   347.3054

Copyright © 1984 by Edward F. Dolan, Jr.
All rights reserved
Printed in the United States of America
5   4   3   2   1

Contents

FOR TIM AND JEANIE

ACKNOWLEDGMENTS

I am indebted to many fine people and organizations for their assistance in the preparation of this book. In particular, for both their continuing help and their making available needed research materials, a special word of thanks must go to attorney Robert Bennett McCreadie; William Royse, formerly of the California Department of Corrections; and Maurice Lafferty, coordinator of the Administration of Justice Program, College of Marin, California. For answering specific questions, I am especially grateful to Nancy Hashimoto, staff member of the Oregon Psychiatric Security Review Board, and to the office of U.S. Representative Barbara Boxer, 6th Congressional District, California; the office of U.S. Senator Orrin Hatch of Utah; and the office of the Subcommittee on the Constitution, an arm of the U.S. Senate Judiciary Committee.

Introduction

For centuries, the courts in all civilized nations have recognized that mentally unbalanced people who are accused of a crime—particularly those who are extremely unbalanced—cannot be treated in the same manner as sane offenders. The sane individual who commits a crime is seen as knowing what he or she was doing and thus is regarded as deserving of punishment. But the same cannot be said of the unbalanced. They may have been so mentally ill when performing a criminal act as not to have been responsible for what they did. It would be unfair, then, to hold them responsible and seek to punish them.

Over the years, this view has resulted in what today is known as the *insanity plea* or the *insanity defense*. Using this plea, an unbalanced offender is able to ask the court to find him or her not guilty of the charged crime—not guilty by reason of insanity.

While the plea is widely regarded as a just one for the

truly unbalanced, it is currently under fire from many quarters in the United States, so much so, in fact, that it has become an issue of stormy and prolonged debate nationwide.

Many Americans, for reasons that we'll see in the coming pages, are questioning the advisability of continuing the use of the plea. They feel that it is being too easily used by many a sane or only mildly unbalanced offender to escape deserved punishment. They want to see it abolished altogether or changed significantly so that such abuses are no longer possible.

Quite as many Americans oppose this viewpoint. While admitting that the plea is, indeed, abused on occasion, they nevertheless believe it to be a fair and just method of legal defense—the *only* fair and just defense for the genuinely and seriously unbalanced person facing the power of the law. The plea, they contend, should be left as it is or should be adjusted in some minor way to safeguard against abuse.

In this book, we're going to look at all aspects of the insanity plea and the American debate it has triggered. We'll study the plea itself to see how it first came into being, how it has been developed over the years, and how it works today. We'll then discuss the reasons for not changing the plea, for abolishing it, and for altering it to one degree or another. We'll conclude with a report on the steps being taken at the federal and state levels to solve the problems surrounding it.

The purpose of doing all this is to help you reach your own decision as to what should be done about the insanity plea so that you can make a contribution to the debate. The contributions of all Americans are needed because the outcome of the debate will determine how the mentally ill are to be treated in courtrooms throughout the nation in the future. It will affect, for better or for worse, the criminal justice system in the United States for generations to come.

[2]

1

The Problem Takes Shape

His name was John W. Hinckley, Jr. He was twenty-five years old, a short, pudgy young man with blondish hair and a pale face. On Monday, March 30, 1981, he stood on a crowded sidewalk in Washington, D.C., near a side entrance of the Hilton Hotel, the entrance reserved for important visitors. Newspaper and television reporters, police officers, government agents, and passers-by stirred excitedly. In just a few moments a very important visitor—the newly elected president of the United States, Ronald Reagan—would come through that entrance. Hinckley's hand went to his coat pocket. His fingers closed over the handle of a .22 caliber revolver.

The hotel was located just five minutes away from the White House by car. President Reagan had arrived early in the afternoon to deliver a brief speech to the 3,500 delegates attending an AFL-CIO labor convention. It was now 2:25 P.M. and the president was due to return to the White House. But if Hinckley had his way, Reagan would never reach his destination. He would never even reach his limousine, which was parked just twenty-five feet (7.6 m) from the entrance. He would be dead before then.

Hinckley stiffened, as did the people around him. He heard the buzz of excited talk. Two of the president's assistants, Press Secretary James Brady and Michael Deaver, the deputy White House chief of staff, came through the door. They hurried across the sidewalk, passing Washington police officer Michael Delahanty as they headed for the car parked just behind Reagan's limousine. Now Hinckley saw the president emerge. Reagan was wearing a dark suit. Walking behind him was Secret Service agent Jerry Parr. Close by was Parr's fellow agent, Timothy McCarthy. President Reagan strode quickly to the limousine's open door.

Near Hinckley, a reporter called to the president, hoping to attract his attention for a question. Hearing the call, Reagan paused at the limousine door, smiled, and raised his arm to wave to the crowd. At that moment, Hinckley chose to act. In one swift movement, he brought the revolver from his pocket, dropped to one knee, and, holding the gun in both hands, took aim and began to fire. The afternoon air crackled with the light popping sounds of the shots. In just two seconds, he emptied the gun of six bullets.

And, in those two seconds, he created havoc. One bullet whistled close to Michael Deaver, missing him by just inches. Another struck Press Secretary Brady in the head and sent him crashing to the pavement. Still another struck police officer Delahanty in the neck. On hearing the shots, agent McCarthy swung in the direction of the sounds and tried to place himself between Hinckley and President Reagan. His face twisted with pain. He went up on his toes and fell forward. A bullet had hit him just below the chest.

President Reagan waves to the crowd
just seconds before the shooting.

Government agents tend to wounded Press
Secretary James Brady and police officer Michael
Delahanty while others restrain John Hinckley.

Startled at the popping noises, Reagan stood for an instant at the limousine's open door. He looked momentarily bewildered. Then Secret Service agent Parr, reacting with lightning-like speed, grabbed the president from behind, doubled him over to reduce his size as a target, and pushed him to safety inside. The door slammed. The long black car sped away.

Perhaps Hinckley had a glimpse of the escaping limousine. Perhaps not. For now the people around him—reporters, police officers, government agents—swarmed over him. They drove him to the pavement and held him pinned there. Others rushed to the aid of the fallen Brady, McCarthy, and Delahanty. Shock and pandemonium reigned along the sidewalk. Shouts filled the air. People yelled for ambulances to be summoned. Minutes later, Hinckley was in handcuffs. Officers herded him into a police car.

Hinckley was the seventh person to have fired on a major public figure in the United States in a period of eighteen years. Lee Harvey Oswald had assassinated President John F. Kennedy in Dallas, Texas, on November 22, 1963. Sirhan B. Sirhan had shot and killed Senator Robert F. Kennedy in 1968. In a sniper attack that same year, James Earl Ray had murdered civil rights leader Martin Luther King, Jr. Arthur Bremer had crippled Alabama Governor George Wallace for life with a bullet fired during the 1972 presidential campaign. Two attempts were made to end the life of President Gerald R. Ford on September 5 and September 12, 1975, by Sara Jane Moore and Lynette Fromme. And, just four months earlier, Mark Chapman had stepped from the shadows at the entrance of New York City's Dakota Apartments and fatally gunned down John Lennon, a former member of the Beatles singing group. Now the latest gunman to assault a major public figure in this country was on his way to a jail cell.

A WOUNDED PRESIDENT

At first no one thought that President Reagan had been harmed in the attack. But then, as the limousine sped toward the White House, the president began to experience difficulty breathing. Agent Parr suspected that the president had broken a rib when being pushed into the car. He ordered the limousine to head for George Washington University Hospital. There, it was learned that Hinckley had come close to succeeding in his assassination attempt. Reagan had indeed been wounded by one of the young man's shots.

It had not been a direct hit. Rather, the bullet had struck the limousine and had ricocheted to enter the president's left side just below the armpit. The bullet had then traveled down his side. It had ricocheted again, this time off a rib, and had punctured his left lung. The slug had finally come to rest a scant 3 inches (7.6 cm) from the president's heart.

On arrival at the hospital, President Reagan underwent surgery. Four hours later, he was in the recovery room. He recuperated over the next two months and returned to his duties at the White House. Miraculously, not one of the other victims of the attack lost his life, though Press Secretary Brady was so badly wounded that, in the hours following the shooting, a rumor flashed through the nation that he had died. Both Secret Service agent McCarthy and police officer Delahanty recovered from their wounds in a matter of weeks. However, Mr. Brady's partial recuperation took many months.

The shootings outraged Americans. The attacks on public figures over recent years were considered a national disgrace. People watched closely as Hinckley was charged with attempted murder. Then, as he awaited trial in a Washington, D.C., federal court, they turned to their newspapers and television sets to learn what kind of man had become the latest to attack a United States president.

A FRIGHTENING PORTRAIT

The picture of Hinckley that emerged was frightening, one of a growing mental unbalance. The Texas-born son of wealthy and respected parents now living near Denver, Colorado, the young man had isolated himself from people over the years and had not given his life any real direction. Seemingly friendless as a teen-ager, he had spent much of his time alone in his room. He had attended Texas Tech University at Lubbock, Texas, on and off for seven years without graduating.

Further, Hinckley had never been able to hold a steady job. Long a fan of the Beatles, he had dreamed of becoming a rock guitarist, singer, and musician. But he had done nothing to turn this ambition into a reality. It had always remained just an idle dream.

Sometime during the years of aimlessness, Hinckley became fascinated with politics. But his interest centered on racist and violent political action. He spent long hours alone reading extremist political literature. He grew to admire Adolf Hitler's Nazi Party, which had destroyed Germany. President Kennedy's killer, Lee Harvey Oswald, became a personal idol.

In 1976, while visiting Hollywood for several months, Hinckley went to see the film *Taxi Driver*. Its central character, a man named Travis Bickle, stalked a political candidate with the intention of killing him. Hinckley's interest in violent political action led to an obsession with the character. He saw the picture no fewer than fifteen times in the next five years. He began to imitate the man and, before long, slipped into the fantasy of thinking that he himself was actually Bickle. He bought guns of the type owned by Bickle. As Bickle had done, he sat in front of a television set and aimed the

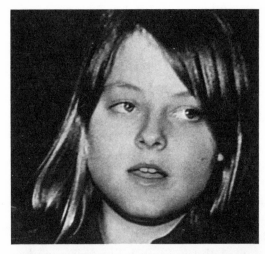

The actress Jodie Foster confirmed that she had received notes and letters signed "John W. Hinckley."

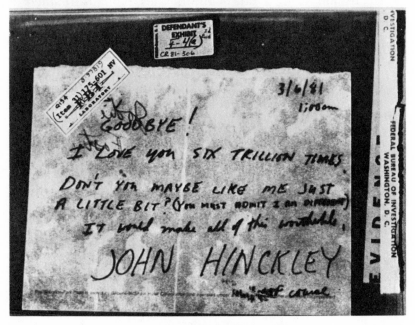

A note written to Jodie Foster, and signed by "John Hinckley," three weeks before President Reagan was shot

guns at the screen. He fell in love with Jodie Foster, the young actress who had played Bickle's girl friend in the film. He wrote poems about her and sent her several love letters.

Out of his fantasy world came the resolve to stalk a public figure just as Bickle had done—and then to assassinate him. He seemed to have three reasons for wanting to kill. He thought it was his destiny to do so. He believed the killing would bring him great fame. And he felt that it would win him Jodie Foster's love and respect. He read books about his idol, Lee Harvey Oswald, and about Sirhan Sirhan. He had photographs taken of himself holding a rifle with a handgun strapped to his waist—photos exactly like those that had been taken of Oswald sometime before President Kennedy's assassination. Hinckley first chose President Jimmy Carter as a target and stalked him for a time. Then he settled on Ronald Reagan and came to the side entrance of the Washington Hilton Hotel on that March afternoon.

THE INSANITY PLEA

Hinckley's trial began in federal court on April 27, 1982, almost fourteen months after the attack. The young man was in federal court because his target had been the chief executive of the federal government. Had the intended victim been an ordinary person in the street, Hinckley would have been tried in a local criminal court in Washington, D.C., since that city, as the scene of the crime, would have had jurisdiction over the case.

On being charged with a criminal offense, defendants must *enter a plea*—that is, declare that they are guilty or not guilty of the charge. When a plea of guilty is entered, a trial does not follow; the defendants simply admit their guilt and give themselves over to what is called the mercy of the court, hoping that the court will

[11]

be lenient in assigning punishment. A plea of not guilty, however, brings a trial. Evidence is presented by the two sides in the case—the prosecution (the side bringing the case against the defendant) and the defense. A jury or, at times, the judge alone makes the final decision as to the defendant's guilt or innocence.

On behalf of their client, Hinckley's attorneys entered a plea of *not guilty by reason of insanity*. This plea is commonly known as either the insanity plea or the insanity defense. Hinckley's lawyers argued that he had been insane at the time he had shot President Reagan. Consequently, he could not be held legally accountable for the attack.

In pleading Hinckley insane, his attorneys were turning to a very old concept in law. The concept requires that two elements be present in a case before a defendant can be found guilty of a crime.

First, it must be shown that the defendant committed an act that is classified in law as a crime. For instance, the taking of a life is always deplorable, but it is a crime only under certain circumstances. It becomes murder when it is done for such reasons as to gain revenge or to get rid of a hated person. A killing, however, is not a crime when it is committed while someone is defending himself or herself against being killed. Thus, a defendant cannot be found guilty and punished if the evidence clearly indicates that he or she was in grave peril and killed in self-defense.

Second, it must be established that the defendant intended to commit a crime.° Let's say that a person is charged with murder. The evidence shows the accused knew murder to be a crime and understood the difference between right and wrong. It then shows that,

°An exception to this would be, however, statutory rape, which is sexual intercourse with a minor. The victim may have consented, but a minor is not judged capable of giving consent.

despite knowing all this, the defendant still went ahead and planned the murder and carried it out. The accused is likely to be found guilty because it is clear that there was *criminal intent*—the resolve to commit an act that is known full well to be a criminal wrong. This defendant would also likely be found guilty if the killing was done in a sudden fit of anger. Even in anger, the accused still knew right from wrong, still knew that he or she was committing a crime, and could have stopped the act.

But, on the other hand, suppose that a person is on trial for shooting and killing one's brother when he came home late one night. The defendant explains to the court that he or she loved the brother and wouldn't have harmed him for the world. It is then explained that the house was dark at the time. The accused saw a person's shadow and was so frightened that it was imagined to be a dangerous attacker. If these facts can be clearly established, the accused can have a strong defense. The defendant neither intended to commit a crime nor knew that he or she was committing one. The element of criminal intent was missing and so the shooting was not a crime but a tragic accident.

Awareness that something one does *might* end in a criminal act is also a factor in criminal intent. Suppose a person drives a car with reckless abandon along a crowded street, and accidently kills a pedestrian. The driver would be charged with a criminal act—perhaps manslaughter—and it will do no good to argue that no harm was intended. A responsible person is expected to be aware that reckless driving is dangerous and that caution is always needed at the wheel. Yet this person elected to drive foolishly. In doing so, the driver showed a willingness—an implied intent—to risk committing a criminal act.

To repeat, both elements—the committing of an

actual crime and the intention to commit a crime—must be shown to be present before a defendant can be found guilty. The insanity plea seeks to defend the accused by removing the element of criminal intent because the defendant, due to a mental defect, lacks the required state of mind to be held responsible for committing the crime. The defendant might have been so insane when strangling a small child that he or she thought the victim to be a laundry bag full of clothing that had somehow come to life. Or an accused might have been so mentally ill that the person no longer knew right from wrong and so did not know it was a crime to kill. Or so ill that the accused couldn't keep from killing one's uncle because "the voice of God inside" said that he was an evil man and so had to be destroyed. In all these instances, it can be argued that the accused was so insane that he or she did not know what was being done. Consequently, the person did not intend to commit a criminal act. With one of the elements of a crime required for conviction now missing, one cannot be found guilty.

TRIAL AND VERDICT

At the time Hinckley's trial began, doctors on the case recognized that the young man was psychotic. But they were not in agreement as to what his exact problem was. There were varied opinions because it remains difficult, even though much is now known about the different forms of insanity, to diagnose the exact nature of a mental illness. In general, however, it was agreed that he was suffering from schizophrenia, an illness that results in a disintegration of the patient's personality and causes him or her to lose contact with the surrounding world.

Using the insanity defense, Hinckley's attorneys freely admitted that he had attacked President Reagan. But, they argued, his mental state at the time of the

[14]

shooting had been such that he had not been in control of his faculties and so could not be held legally accountable for what he had done. They brought to the witness stand a number of psychiatrists who testified that Hinckley had, indeed, been insane that terrible afternoon. One told the jury that the young man had been so filled with "inner rages" and had been sinking so deeply into his "fantasies" that he had a sense of "losing control" of himself.

The prosecuting attorneys agreed that Hinckley was mentally disturbed. But they contended he had not been so insane that he had not known the wrongness of what he was doing on that March day. They brought psychiatrists of their own to the witness stand to back up their arguments. One testified that "John was never so disturbed or distraught that he was unaware of what he was doing."

Watched closely by the entire nation, the trial ran for eight weeks. In mid-June, the jury left the courtroom to discuss the evidence and reach a verdict. They returned on June 21, three and a half days later. The verdict: John W. Hinckley, Jr., was innocent of the charges on the grounds of insanity.

Once the verdict was rendered, the judge faced a difficult decision. Believing Hinckley to have been insane at the time of the shooting, the jury had acquitted the young man. Had the case concerned a sane defendant, who was found not guilty, he would now have to be set free. But could this be done with Hinckley? Was his insanity a temporary or a permanent condition? If temporary, was he still so unbalanced that he was a danger to both society and himself? Should he be placed for treatment in a mental institution? Or, in the months since March 30, 1981, had he recovered to the point where he was no longer a threat and thus was entitled to his freedom? It was up to the judge to decide. Under federal law, he had fifty days in which to find an answer.

Hinckley was placed in St. Elizabeths Hospital, a mental institution in Washington, D.C., while the matter was being settled. In reaching a decision, the judge listened to arguments from both the prosecuting and defense attorneys. The prosecuting attorneys, who had once contended that Hinckley had known what he was doing that March 30, now argued that he was insane enough to require confinement in a mental facility. The defense attorneys felt that their client's mental condition remained hazardous. They said they would not argue for his freedom until he was "no longer a danger to himself or society." In the end, the judge decreed that Hinckley was not to be set free. The young man was to stay at St. Elizabeths and be given psychiatric treatment. Hinckley remains there to this day.

THE CONTROVERSY

Long before they had ever heard of John W. Hinckley, Jr., many Americans had been troubled over the insanity plea. Originating in England, the plea was a well-established point in U.S. law. It was an outgrowth of a philosophy that the courts of most nations have recognized for centuries: that it is unfair to treat an insane defendant as you would a sane one. But countless Americans, while appreciating its intent, saw the plea as a convenient loophole through which many guilty offenders could jump to escape a deserved punishment. Some, though mentally disturbed, could use the loophole when they really weren't all *that* insane. Others needed only to pretend insanity well enough to fool the courts and the psychiatrists. In either instance, they could set themselves up to be freed or sent to a mental institution. They escaped the hardships of imprisonment.

The Hinckley verdict shocked and outraged all the Americans who disliked the plea, plus millions more who had never before given it a thought. The shock and outrage stemmed from three points. First, there hadn't been any doubt whatsoever about the fact that he had committed a crime. The people around him had seen him fire the shots. He himself and his attorneys had admitted the shooting. Yet he had been found innocent on many saw as a technicality—a convenient loophole. Had he not been confined to St. Elizabeths, he would have been set free, perhaps to kill again. While most people recognized that Hinckley's background and behavior indicated mental unbalance, they still felt that justice had not been done. His guilt was so obvious that, no matter the degree of his insanity, he should have been sentenced and imprisoned. While serving his sentence, he could have been given psychiatric care.

The second point troubled some people even more. They felt they were living in an age that treated criminals with an increasing leniency, a dangerous leniency that did nothing but invite more crime. Widespread in the country was the belief that too many genuinely guilty offenders were released not on the merits of their cases but on such legal defenses as the plea. And there was also the belief that, in the words of so many Americans, criminals got no more than a "slap on the wrist" from the law when they went to court. The Hinckley verdict struck them as just one more indication of that growing leniency.

It was a verdict, after all, that not only kept the young man out of prison but also, now that he was confined to St. Elizabeths, gave him a good chance to go free in a very short time. His case had been tried under federal law, which now permitted him to ask for his release from the hospital about every six months. His request would go before a judge and, if the hospital psychiatrists reported him again well enough to require no further confinement, the judge might well decide to set him free. And then what might happen? Might he go out of his mind again? Might he have fooled the psychiatrists? Might he begin to stalk President Reagan once more? Might he kill again?

The third reason for public concern centered on the national attention that had been given the Hinckley case. As would not have been true of a minor and little-known trial, millions were aware that Hinckley had escaped punishment with the insanity plea. Wouldn't that encourage an even greater number of sane criminals to try to hide behind it? And wouldn't some unbalanced people, even though sane enough to know right from wrong, be encouraged to attempt crimes that they wouldn't have committed in the past? An aide to President Reagan echoed these fears when he told the press that now "every cuckoo in the world" might decide it was perfectly safe to take a shot at the chief executive. The nation could well be hit with an epidemic of senseless crimes, all in the name of insanity.

As a result of these varied concerns, the insanity plea, which had bothered many Americans over the years, suddenly became an issue of stormy national debate. It was a debate that revolved about a single question: Just what should the country do about the plea? Public opinion quickly divided itself along three lines over the answer.

Many people felt that the only solution was to abolish the plea as a legal defense in all the courts of the land; it was too fraught with danger ever to be permitted again. At the opposite end of the opinion scale were those who believed that the plea should be left as it is. It contained dangers, yes, but it was the only one that was fair to defendants not in full possession of their senses. They were ill and needed to be treated as such. It would be grossly unjust to punish them as one would punish a sane offender.

Finally, there were many people who took a middle-of-the-road approach. Agreeing that the plea was necessary, they saw it, at the same time, as a dangerous legal loophole. Their answer: Rather than abolish the plea, they wanted it revised in some way to prevent truly sane offenders from taking advantage of it.

And so the lines for a new national debate were drawn. In the next chapters, we're going to look at the debate in all its aspects. We'll consider the reasons for abolishing the insanity plea, for altering it in some way, and for leaving it as is. Then we'll discuss the steps being taken at the national and state levels to solve the problem. But, before we can do any of these things, we must look further at the plea itself to see exactly what it involves.

2

The Insanity Plea: A History

We will look at the insanity plea in two steps. First, in this chapter, we'll examine its history and see how it came into being. Then, because it has been changed over the years, in Chapter Three we'll examine the plea as it is today.

One point has to be made regarding the story of the plea as told in this chapter. Over the centuries, virtually all nations have developed their own special ways of dealing with insanity cases. But the history in this chapter is drawn almost solely from Great Britain, where the view of our American courts toward insanity cases originated.

THE BEGINNINGS
Suppose that you lived in ancient times, got into trouble with the law, and were taken to trial. And suppose that you were mentally unbalanced. The courts in most countries would not give you special treatment because of your problem. Regardless of your mental state, you

would be judged either innocent or guilty on the facts of whether you did or did not commit the offense. Nor would you be given special treatment if found guilty. You would be punished in the same way that a sane person would be punished.

For the most part, this approach was used because ancient societies had virtually no scientific knowledge whatsoever of mental illnesses, their various types, and the degrees to which they can affect people. There simply were not enough facts at hand for the courts to take insanity into account as a factor in a crime. But, were you to get into trouble some centuries later and be sent to trial, you would find that the situation was changing. Although mental illness was still much of a mystery, judges and attorneys throughout the world were beginning to recognize one point. They could see that some unbalanced people were much like very young children and thus deserved special consideration.

As remains true to this day, very young children who committed crimes were not held legally responsible for them. The reason: The youngsters had not yet reached what was called "the age of use of reason," which was customarily set at around seven years of age (in modern times it varies from place to place, with the courts also taking into consideration such factors as the child's intelligence and degree of maturity). Children under the age of seven were neither taken to court nor punished because they were regarded as being too immature to have known that they were committing a crime. They had not yet learned right from wrong. Missing from their actions was the element of criminal intent. The courts could see that some unbalanced people—those who were extremely unbalanced— might have been so out of touch with reality that they, too, might not have realized that they were doing something wrong. Hence, it was only fair to treat them as though they were very young children. They needed to be given special consideration. People who were born mentally defective or who became mentally defective through accident or illness were seen as needing the same consideration.

AN EARLY CONSIDERATION

A good example of this special consideration was to be seen in England early in the thirteenth century. There, as in ancient societies, the court did not take your insanity into consideration during your trial; as usual, you were judged innocent or guilty solely on the facts of whether you actually committed the offense or not. The special consideration came into play after the trial if you were found guilty. You were allowed to turn to the king for help. If he wished, he could grant you a pardon so that you need not serve a prison sentence or be executed.

Later in the century, a special verdict was developed for insane or mentally defective defendants who were charged with murder. If they were judged guilty, the new verdict made a pardon by the king almost automatic.

By the fourteenth century, the English courts were beginning to consider insanity during trials, especially those having to do with murder or some other violent crime that called for the death penalty. Insanity was coming to be seen as a legitimate legal defense that could be used by your attorney to protect you from being found guilty in the first place. But if the jury found you guilty anyway, the judge could spare you from execution. Your property, however, would most likely be taken from you.

As soon as a consideration of insanity was allowed during trials, the English courts came up against a problem. Even though little was yet known of mental illness, anyone could see that insanity came in varying degrees. It seemed obvious that those defendants who were just slightly unbalanced deserved to be held accountable for their crimes. Like the child who had reached the age of use of reason, they appeared sensible enough to have known they were doing a wrong. It could be presumed, then, that they could harbor criminal intent. So just how mentally unbalanced did a person need to be before he or she could justifiably turn to insanity as a legal defense?

"ABSOLUTE MADNESS"

The courts answered this question with what they called "absolute madness." In time, it came to be known as a *complete legal defense*. This meant that you could not be held in any degree responsible if your attorney could successfully demonstrate in court that you had been "absolutely" mad at the time the crime was committed. Being "absolutely" mad, you couldn't possibly have harbored criminal intent. You had to be found guiltless. The court had no other choice.

But the idea of absolute madness presented a problem. It was too general a term for practical purposes. It obviously indicated a total or almost total loss of the mind. But before absolute madness could be intelligently argued and judged in court, its exact meaning had to be spelled out. Otherwise, there would be confusion, with everyone using the same term but with each person, in his own mind, having a slightly different meaning for it. Until there was a precise definition, no one could expect juries to hand down equitable verdicts.

In an attempt to clear up the matter, various definitions were developed over the years. For instance, a prominent British judge of the fourteenth century said that an absolute "madman is one who does not know what he is doing, who lacks in mind and reason, and is not far removed from the brutes." Two centuries later, a London attorney named William Lombard advised that insanity cases be decided on the question of whether the defendant is a reasonably sensible person or "a natural fool or a lunatic or a child who apparently has no knowledge of good or evil." If a fool, a lunatic, or a child, then the person should not be convicted because he or she was without "any understanding will" to guide his or her actions at the time of the crime.

In themselves, these definitions were almost hopelessly vague. But, at their base—and at the base of others made through the years—was the idea that defendants could be excused from responsibility only if they were so unbalanced at the time of their offense that they had not known, in Lombard's words, "good from evil." In time, these words were changed to "right and wrong." This concept—being able to differentiate between right and wrong—served as the basic guide in judging insanity cases through the next centuries and became a part of what is known as English common law.

(English common law is a broad body of basic laws developed over the centuries as the British people tried to solve the various legal problems that came their way. In great part, it is a traditional and unwritten body of law that underlies all the laws that England has since put into writing. It is called a "judge-made law" because it was developed as judges made decisions in individual cases. The decisions rendered in individual cases then served as guides—as *precedents*—for the decisions made in later, similar cases. English common law was brought to the United States by the first colonists and to this day serves as the basis for much American law.)

THE NEXT STEP

The next major step in the development of the insanity plea was taken in England during the 1840s. Early in that decade, a man named Daniel M'Naghton set out to assassinate Sir Robert Peel, the British prime minister. Standing at curbside as a procession of government carriages rolled past, M'Naghton pulled a revolver from his pocket and fired at the carriage in which Peel always rode. The bullet struck its target, killing him instantly, but the victim turned out to be not Peel but his private secretary. Peel's life was spared because Queen Victoria, who had been scheduled to participate in the procession, was away on other business. At the last moment, the prime minister had decided to ride in her carriage.

Apprehended at the scene, M'Naghton was charged with murder and placed on trial. His lawyer argued that M'Naghton should be found not guilty on the grounds that the man had been insane at the time of the shooting. But the attorney did not base his argument on the old idea that his client had been so deranged as not to have known right from wrong. Rather, he contended that M'Naghton had been the victim of mad delusions. M'Naghton, he said, had wildly imagined that he was being persecuted and tormented by a number of people, chief among them the prime minister. Helpless in the grip of his fantasies, he had set out to put an end to his "persecution."

This argument deeply impressed the jurors. They acquitted M'Naghton of the murder charge on the grounds of insanity. As would happen more than a century later in the wake of the Hinckley trial, the verdict triggered widespread public outrage—and for the same reasons. M'Naghton was obviously guilty. The people near him at curbside had seen him fire the fatal shot. He had tried to kill a major public figure. He deserved to be punished. Yet he had gotten off scot-free. Additionally, England was as politically troubled at the time as the United States was to be in the years before the Hinckley shooting. Several attempts had been made on the life of Queen Victoria. The verdict, people felt certain, would lead to further attempts.

As a result of the public outcry, Britain's House of Lords asked fifteen of the nation's most distinguished judges to review the verdict and comment on it with the aim of setting firm standards for judging insanity cases in the future. Out of their deliberations came what has been known ever since as the *M'Naghton Rule*. It stated more clearly the grounds for judging insanity cases than did the idea of "absolute madness" and thus became the chief guide used in future trials.

The rule was stated in the final report that the judges submitted to the House of Lords. They stated that the courts should require an attorney to establish either of two points when defending a client on the grounds of insanity.

They called, first, for the attorney to show that the defendant was suffering so severely from a "defect of reason" resulting from a "disease of the mind" that he or she did not understand "the nature and quality of the act" being committed. In nonlegal language, the defendant had to be so ill as not to have known what he or she was doing. For a simple illustration of what was meant here, the judges turned to the case of the man who hacked a relative to death with an axe while thinking that he was chopping down a tree.

Next, the judges considered the defendant who, though unbalanced, might still have some idea of the act being committed. Here, they fell back on the old idea of knowing right from wrong. The attorney, they said, now had to show that the defendant—again by reason of a defect resulting from a disease of the mind—did not recognize that what he or she was doing was wrong in the eyes of the law.

M'Naghton's attorney, in arguing that his client had been driven to murder by wild delusions, had intro-

Daniel M'Naghton on trial for murder in England

duced a new wrinkle into insanity trials. For the first time, diseases of the mind were being seriously studied in England, and M'Naghton's attorney had used a recently published and highly respected medical-legal textbook, *Medical Jurisprudence in Insanity*, to back up his arguments and impress the jurors. Since, under common law, the decisions reached in current trials would serve as guides to future courtroom decisions, the fifteen judges knew that delusions would be an issue in later cases. This brought them to their next point. They realized that the courts now had to have some way of measuring which delusions deserved to see defendants acquitted and which deserved to see them punished.

They came up with what seemed to be a simple solution. They wrote that a defendant who acted under an insane delusion but was not otherwise insane, must be judged according to the facts of the offense as they seemed to him or her. The judges used two examples to explain what was meant here. First, suppose that a man suffers from the delusion that his neighbor is trying to murder him; he kills the neighbor in what he imagines to be self-defense; he is to be judged guiltless. But suppose that the man wildly imagines that the neighbor is saying ugly things about him and is attempting to destroy his good name; he kills the neighbor in revenge; he is now open to be found guilty and punished.

Obviously, in this section of the M'Naghton Rule, the judges were applying to the mentally unbalanced defendant a point in law that had always applied to the sane person. As you know, a killing in self-defense, if proved to be such, leaves the sane defendant blameless, whereas a killing for revenge is never permitted and, if proved to be such, will see the sane defendant judged guilty. For the insane defendant, the delusion itself was not a factor. It was rather the nature of the defendant's intent while suffering the delusion that must be considered.

The M'Naghton Rule became a part of English common law and, as did all earlier English common law, found its way to the United States. It was followed in American courts for years. However, as psychiatric studies in the twentieth century told us more and more about the complex nature of mental illness, the rule began to be severely criticized. Medicine and the courts came to realize that a wide variety of diseases and defects could impair the mind and lead their victims to criminal acts. The M'Naghton Rule was neither broad enough in scope to take them all into consideration nor flexible enough to ensure that such defendants would all be fairly handled in court.

For instance, there was the matter of delusions. Many a legal expert thought it unfair to apply to their victims a point of law that was applied to a sane defendant. Further, there was the matter of what had been found by psychiatric research to be "irresistible impulses"— wild inner urges that could lead to criminal acts, urges of such magnitude that the sufferer seemed incapable of disobeying them. Because the M'Naghton Rule had been written before these impulses were really known, it did not seem to take them into consideration at all.

Clearly, a new and broader rule was needed. For a time in the 1950s, the U.S. courts tried working with the rule that a defendant was not to be found responsible "if his unlawful act was the product of a mental disease or defect." But the wording here was much too general. Juries were left without any real guidelines as to what degree of mental illness would separate the innocent from the guilty.

In the 1960s, the American Law Institute formulated a new rule. Proving satisfactory to both the medical and legal professions, it has replaced the M'Naghton Rule and has been made a part of federal law and the laws in many states. It is the rule that brings us to the insanity plea as it is today.

3

The Insanity Plea: Today

The American Law Institute (ALI) rule calls for defendants to be judged insane and found guiltless if either of two points can be satisfactorily established in court. It must be shown that, as a result of a mental disease or mental defect, they lacked at the time of their offense the substantial mental capacity either (1) to appreciate the criminality (the wrongfulness) of their conduct *or* (2) to conform their conduct to the requirements of the law.

On the surface, the ALI rule seems very similar to the M'Naghton Rule—and in some respects it is. The inability of the defendants "to appreciate the criminality of their conduct" contains the old idea of being unable to differentiate between right and wrong. And the defendants' inability "to conform their conduct to the requirements of the law" covers those offenders who were so ill that they did not know what they were doing—did not, as the M'Naghton Rule put it, understand "the nature and quality" of their act. Further, both rules take into account not only the mentally unbalanced but also the person who is born mentally defective or becomes mentally defective through accident or illness. The wording in both rules refers to "mental disease or defect."

THE DIFFERENCES

But here the similarity ends. The M'Naghton Rule was criticized for being too narrow in scope and too inflexible, especially in the area of judging defendants who suffered delusions. Under M'Naghton, remember, you would most likely be found guilty if your delusion led you to a revenge killing but innocent if it tricked you into killing in self-defense. The ALI rule is much broader and far more flexible because, in referring to defendants who are unable "to conform their conduct to the requirements of the law," it takes in all the people that McNaghton did not really cover—all those people whose derangements cause them to lose such control of themselves that, even if they do have some glimmering of right and wrong, they cannot stop themselves from doing wrong. Included here, of course, are the victims of overwhelming delusions and the schizophrenics whose fantasies have taken over their lives. Now, were you on trial for something done under a delusion, the nature of what you did would not dictate how you were to be judged. Judgment, rather, would be on the severity of the delusion.

Also included here are the victims of "irresistible impulses." You'll recall that, like delusions, irresistible impulses are wild and groundless imaginings. They are overpowering urges to take an action, so overpowering that they cannot be disobeyed. In Chapter One, we spoke of how you might be driven to kill your uncle because "the voice of God inside you" ordered you to do so. That was just one very simple example of an irresistible impulse.

As was mentioned in Chapter Two, the M'Naghton Rule, because it was written when little was known of them, did not go into the matter of irresistible impulses. But, since they seem so much like delusions, it can be presumed that they were to be handled in the same way, with judgment based on whether or not the act committed in their name added up to a crime. The flexible ALI rule enables the decision to be made on the power of the impulse itself rather than on the nature of the act resulting from it.

The concept of the irresistible impulse, however, is one that a number of courts in the United States frown upon. It is accepted as an insanity defense under federal law and in many states. But it is not recognized in several states. The courts in these states believe that irresistible impulses can be too easily employed by the offender who deliberately started out to commit a crime and was not, in fact, driven to it.

As flexible as the ALI rule is, it contains one basic point that is inflexible and cannot be altered. The insanity plea requires that the defendant be suffering his or her loss of mind at the time the criminal act is committed. Were you the defendant, it would not count if you became unbalanced at some time after committing the crime. You would still be held responsible because you were in your right mind and knew what you were doing when you got into trouble. For the same reason, it would not count if you were unbalanced at some time beforehand but then regained your senses in time for the act. Further, if you fully or partially recovered by the time of your trial, you could still plead insanity. All that counts is your mental state at the time of the criminal act. This is a fundamental point of logic that can be found in the laws of all the countries using the insanity defense. It dates far back over the centuries.

DIMINISHED CAPACITY

The overall flexibility of the ALI rule makes it possible to include the matter of *diminished capacity* in insanity cases. This concept, which is presently recognized in only a few states, is a modern one in law and springs from the twentieth century's growing knowledge of mental illness. Briefly, the term means "partial insanity." Taken into consideration here is the fact that a person may be able to reason sanely in some areas of life but not in other areas. That such a person, though not totally insane, is unbalanced in one area may serve to make him or her less guilty of a crime.

To understand how diminished capacity works, we have to return to a point made in Chapter One. You'll remember that, if you're to be judged guilty of a crime, two elements must be established: first, that you committed an act classified as a crime and, second, that you harbored a criminal intent in the performance of the act. Now let's say that your employer has been making your life miserable for a long while, perhaps constantly badgering you, perhaps cheating you of your wages. Unable to stand things any longer, you've killed him in a fit of anger and have been charged with first-degree murder.

For you to be found guilty of that particular charge, it will have to be shown in court that, as part of your criminal intent, the killing was *premeditated*. This means that, in your right mind, you deliberately planned to do away with your boss and then deliberately did so. You'll be able to defend yourself if you can show that your diminished capacity—your imbalance—was such that it rendered you incapable of premeditation. Though quite sane in other areas of your life, you were so upset in this one area—your terrible relations with your boss—that you hadn't the wit to plan the killing but lost your reason and went about it in a sudden, mad rage.

[33]

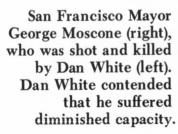

San Francisco Mayor
George Moscone (right),
who was shot and killed
by Dan White (left).
Dan White contended
that he suffered
diminished capacity.

To look at your case from another angle, a charge of first-degree murder also requires that you, again as part of your criminal intent, kill with *malice aforethought*. This legal term—which means "planning to do harm without excuse or legal justification"—stems from the age-old understanding by all societies that people must be allowed to live in safety and that no one may set out to hurt them for such malicious reasons as hatred, revenge, or sadistic pleasure. Again, you can defend yourself if you can demonstrate that, because of diminished capacity, you were so mentally ill in one area of your life that you did not grasp society's rule about not deliberately and maliciously injuring others. Consequently, you could not have harbored malice aforethought.

Since diminished capacity admits that you are only partially insane, it also admits that you are partially guilty. Consequently, it is not a defense that permits acquittal as can happen with the insanity plea itself. Rather, it allows you to admit to the act and then seek a lesser charge because you are only partially guilty of the act. It may, for instance, allow the charge to be reduced from first-degree murder to second-degree murder or manslaughter, each of which brings less punishment.

A well-known case of diminished capacity resulting in a lesser charge occurred some years ago in San Francisco, California. On November 27, 1978, a young political leader in the city, Dan White, entered City Hall and made his way, in turn, to the offices of Mayor George Moscone and City Supervisor Harvey Milk. He shot and killed both men. When he turned himself in to the authorities, White contended that he had been suffering diminished capacity because of the tremendous personal, financial, and political strains that had been placed on him during the months before the shootings. He was eventually found guilty not of first-degree murder but of manslaughter and was sentenced to a term of seven years and eight months in California's Soledad State Prison. As this book is being written, his parole is being considered.

INSANITY TRIALS

When you are on trial for a crime, the law states that you cannot be justifiably convicted unless the trial proves you to be, in the words of the law, *guilty beyond a reasonable doubt*. Even if the jurors strongly suspect you, they're not supposed to bring in a guilty verdict if there is the least shadow of doubt in their minds. This rule is a long-standing one in law and is, of course, intended to protect everyone from guesswork verdicts that could send the innocent to prison.

The job of proving guilt beyond a reasonable doubt is called the *burden of proof*. Most people think that establishing the burden of proof is the responsibility of the prosecution attorneys. The feeling is that, since they are responsible for bringing the case against you, they must then be the ones to prove you guilty. While this holds true in most all criminal trials, it is not necessarily true in insanity cases.

The side—prosecution or defense—responsible for establishing the burden of proof of your guilt or innocence in an insanity trial is determined by federal or state law. In a federal trial, as was John Hinckley's, the burden lies with the prosecution attorneys. It's their job to answer your insanity plea by proving that you were sane at the time of the crime and thus are guilty as charged; the defense, presenting evidence showing that you may well have been insane, tries to create enough of a shadow of doubt to keep the jurors from declaring you guilty. This same arrangement is used in many states, but there are a number of states—California among them—that place the burden of proof with you and require your attorneys to prove you innocent.

These states want things done this way because, with the insanity plea, you're admitting to the crime but are demanding that very special circumstances be taken into consideration to find you innocent. It's a demand that these states say cannot be lightly made. They will not allow you to claim that you are insane and then sit back and let the prosecution try to prove the opposite. Instead, *your* attorneys must prove the validity of your claim. This is done by demonstrating that a *preponderance of the evidence*—the main weight of the evidence presented in court—is in your favor. As for the prosecution, it now tries to show that you were in your right mind so that a shadow of doubt is raised about your claim.

The jurors in the Hinckley trial were roundly criticized by great segments of the public and press for their not-guilty verdict. But there were many legal experts—and many people from all walks of life—who said that the jurors had reached a correct decision. The jurors knew that, under federal law, the prosecution bore the burden of proof. Faced with a strong defense, the prosecution had been unable to prove beyond all doubt that the young man had been sane at the time he injured President Reagan and three others. The jury, then, had no choice but to find him innocent by reason of insanity.

When reading news accounts of such trials as Hinckley's, you'll often see the insanity plea referred to as a *special defense*. For many people, the term has a mysterious ring to it, but its meaning is quite simple. All criminal cases involve either of two basic defenses—*general* or *special*. Should you plead not guilty to a murder on the grounds that you simply did not commit it (claiming, perhaps, that you were miles away from the scene at the time), you'll be employing a general defense. But, as soon as you admit to the killing and then argue that special circumstances—anything from self-defense to insanity—actually make you innocent of it, then you are using a special defense.

Though the insanity plea is a special defense, a claim of diminished capacity is not. It comes under the category of a general defense because you are not asking to be found totally innocent for special circumstances. Rather, because diminished capacity adds up to partial insanity, you are asking to be found only partially guilty and thus to be charged with a lesser crime and given the lighter sentence that it brings.

AFTER THE TRIAL

Now, what happens at the end of your trial? What happens if you're found innocent? If you're found guilty?

Should the verdict be not guilty, you'll almost always, as was John Hinckley, be placed in a mental hospital or institution so that you can be given psychiatric care. The great majority of not-guilty verdicts end in this manner. However, if such confinement is not seen as needed, you'll then likely be placed under medical supervision on an out-patient basis and will have to report regularly, even daily, for treatment with a psychiatrist or psychologist; you may continue as an out-patient for months, years, or even the rest of your life; it all depends on your condition. Should you be placed in a mental hospital or institution, you'll be held there until judged well enough to be safely released. On release, you, too, will probably be placed under medical supervision on an out-patient basis.

You may be released all at once or a step at a time. If the latter, you may be allowed to leave the institution on occasion for several hours or several days to visit relatives or friends. You may be freed for a number of hours daily so that you can take a job. All this is meant to help you return more easily to normal life.

If, like Hinckley, you are confined for care under federal law, you'll be entitled to petition for release about every six months. A court hearing will be required to determine your fate. Evidence will be presented to the court by the hospital psychiatrists and psychologists and by your attorney as to your present state of mind and your progress toward recovery. There may be disagreement among the parties presenting the evidence, with some saying that you should be released and others recommending your continued confinement. It will be up to the judge or a jury to weigh all the evidence, consider the recommendations, and then decide whether you're fit for a safe release.

You may also petition for release periodically when you are judged innocent and then confined for care by a state court. But the times for petitioning vary among the states. Some states go along with federal law and allow a petition about every six months. Others may demand a longer period between petitions, perhaps a year or more. Your petition may be considered by a judge alone or by a jury.

In some states, the handling of insanity cases is considered a medical rather than a legal matter. Their laws enable the mental hospital or institution to release you on its own authority. No court hearing or order is required.

Depending on your improvement, you may spend less time in confinement for care than you would have spent in prison had you been found guilty. It's also possible that you'll be confined for a much longer period, perhaps even for life. This is what happened to two men—Richard Lawrence and John Schrank—who attempted presidential assassinations many years ago.

In 1835, Lawrence attempted to assassinate President Andrew Jackson, only to have his pistol misfire. At his trial, the demented Lawrence claimed that he was King Richard III of England; he was placed in an asylum for the rest of his life. John Schrank wounded Theodore Roosevelt with a bullet in 1912 while the former presi-

Richard Lawrence attempted to
kill President Andrew Jackson.

dent was campaigning for another term in the White House. On claiming that he had been ordered to shoot Roosevelt by President William McKinley's ghost, Schrank was ordered to a mental institution. He died there thirty-one years later.

Though it is possible that you may be confined for care for the rest of your life, it is more likely that you will one day be released. In long years past, confinement almost invariably meant a lifetime in an asylum, as it did for Lawrence and Schrank. But, as more and more has been learned about treating the mentally ill, the situation has been changing. Especially in the past two decades or so, the mental-care system in the United States—along with much American insanity law—has turned away from simply locking up patients and has tried to rehabilitate them so they might become useful citizens. Consequently, it is considered unjust to hold in further confinement patients who have been rehabilitated to the point where they appear no longer dangerous and thus seem entitled to the chance for a normal life. This is why federal law and the laws in some states give patients the right to petition periodically for release and why other states allow mental facilities to release a patient on their own authority.

As we'll see in the next chapter, the people who oppose the insanity plea see grave risks in the release of such patients. Their chief fear about the use of the plea is that many violent offenders may be released, only to do new violence.

Now let's look at the opposite side of the coin and say that, despite your plea of insanity, you are judged guilty. You will then receive a prison sentence just as a sane offender would. While serving your sentence, you will likely receive psychiatric care. Depending on the facilities available, you may be housed in a special area at the prison if your unbalance is severe enough. Or you may be assigned to a mental hospital or institution.

Once your sentence is served, you may face any of several fates. You may be released. You may be held in a psychiatric facility for further treatment until deemed well enough for freedom. Or you may be placed under medical supervision on an out-patient basis. Everything here depends on the laws involved (federal or state), the circumstances of your case, and the dangers of your mental condition to yourself and others.

These, then, are the basic facts surrounding the insanity plea. It's time now to look at the arguments for and against the plea. We'll begin with those against its continued use.

4

Against the Plea

Surveys of public opinion indicate that the majority of Americans dislike the insanity plea and want to see it discarded altogether or changed in some manner. For instance, a poll taken in the autumn of 1981 by the Associated Press and the news division of the National Broadcasting Company (NBC) showed that 69 percent of the people questioned felt that the plea should at least be barred from murder trials. The poll also revealed that 87 percent of the people questioned feared that too many accused murderers turn to the plea to avoid being sent to prison.

What exactly are the reasons why so many Americans dislike and fear the insanity plea?

FREED TO DO NEW VIOLENCE
As was mentioned in Chapter Three, the greatest fear seems to be that, in the wake of a not-guilty verdict, violent offenders will be unwisely released from confinement for care and will possibly commit new vio-

lences. Just how widely that fear is felt can be seen in a 1982 survey that was conducted by the American Broadcasting Company (ABC) following the Hinckley trial. The great majority of people said that Hinckley should not be released from St. Elizabeths Hospital. But 78 percent believed that he would one day be set free.

The opponents of the plea say that the fear of unwise release is a valid and not an imagined one. As proof, they point to the terrible crimes—from beatings to rape to murder—that have already followed some releases.

For example, there is the case of Robert E. Miller of Hawaii. In a 1973 sniper attack, he shot and killed a woman as she stood in the window of her home. The woman was a perfect stranger to him. Judged guilty by reason of insanity, Miller was confined to a state mental hospital, where he remained for six years until the doctors believed him well enough to be granted a leave of absence for several days. Miller immediately returned to the neighborhood of the shooting. He obtained a rifle and a short time later felled six tourists in another senseless sniper attack.

The opponents of the plea believe that there are a number of circumstances in effect today that highly favor the unwise release of such dangerous patients as Miller. To begin, there is the already-mentioned policy of the U.S. mental care system to rehabilitate patients rather than hold them for a lifetime. It's a policy that is bringing about an increasing number of releases. Some of them are merited. But some of them are tragically undeserved.

Second, the law today tends to regard mental patients with criminal backgrounds in the same light as patients who have no history of crime. As part of the civil rights protections granted everyone against unjust imprisonment, the law requires that patients without criminal backgrounds be released as soon as they are judged well again. They are sane and innocent of wrongdoing and so cannot be held against their will. It is this same requirement that gives you, the recovering patient *with* a criminal background, the right to petition a court periodically for release if you live in a state where court permission is needed. Or to petition the hospital directly if your state delegates such responsibility to the hospital.

Further, should you be in a state requiring a court petition, your request, as you know, will be decided by a judge or a jury. The hospital staff may advise against the release. But they can do nothing if overruled for some reason by the judge or jury. You must be freed, at least on an out-patient basis. You're legally presumed sane again. By virtue of having been earlier acquitted on the grounds of insanity, you're innocent of a crime. You cannot be held against your will.

The same rules apply to release by the hospital itself. Even if some staff members object, you must be released if the majority opinion, though perhaps mistaken, holds you to be sufficiently well once more.

Another consideration is the presence in today's market of what are called psychotropic drugs. These medications, which were unknown a quarter century ago, are used in the treatment of various mental illnesses. They do not cure the illnesses. Rather, they often cause them to go into remission. This means that, were you a patient who took a psychotropic medication, the outward symptoms of your illness would disappear and you would behave normally again. You'd go on behaving more or less normally for as long as you took the medication. But should its use be stopped, your old behavior—irrational and perhaps violent—would quickly return.

The danger here, obviously, is that you'll appear so normal as to win a release, only to stop using the medication when you are free. Perhaps you'll convince a judge or jury that all is well. Perhaps the hospital, thinking that you can now be treated with medication on an out-patient basis, will support your court petition or, if state laws permit, will itself release you. What then happens if you disappear and stop the medication?

As the opponents of the plea see it, any combination of these circumstances can create a lethal situation. Two recent cases certainly support this view. Both were reported in a 1983 television program that NBC presented on insanity and the law.

In the first, a man known to have committed ten murders was judged not guilty by reason of insanity. He was sent to a state mental hospital and remained there for several years. At last, claiming to be well again, he appealed for release. Believing that he was still very ill, the hospital staff recommended against the petition. But the jury was persuaded by the man's attorney and decided against the recommendation. The hospital had no choice but to set him free. A month later, he beat his wife to death.

The second case involved a man who was taking psychotropic medication. He was released because he had been behaving normally for close to a year. Once he was at home, he stopped the medication. He began to imagine that a neighbor upstairs wanted to drink his blood. The result: He stabbed the neighbor to death.

U.S. Senator Orrin Hatch (Republican, Utah) is among the national political leaders who are critical of the insanity plea. He is seeking to have Congress abolish the insanity defense from federal law and replace it with a new defense (we'll be talking about his proposal in a later chapter). Much of his criticism of the plea centers on the federal and state laws that have sprung up around it in recent years. He gives his views in an article, "The Insanity Defense Is Insane," that he wrote for a 1982 issue of *Reader's Digest.*

U.S. Senator Orrin Hatch is critical
of the insanity plea.

The senator argues that these laws have made it increasingly difficult to handle the confinement of defendants acquitted as insane. He is not only talking here about the hearings required before there can be confinement or about the periodic petitions for release. He writes that some states now call for court permission to transfer a patient from one institution to another if he or she objects to the move. In some states, patients have the right to go to court if they do not like the medication or treatment being administered to them.

All these laws involve time-consuming courtroom procedures. They pose problems for court calendars that are often already overcrowded. Life is made more complicated for both judges and medical people. All this—plus many other factors, among them the fact that so many mental hospitals are filled to capacity today—has created a great pressure to release patients. Releasing them seems to be less burdensome than treating them on an out-patient basis.

DIFFICULT TO EVALUATE
THE INSANE

Senator Hatch's article also points to the second great fear surrounding the insanity plea. Along with all the other circumstances that can lead to unwise releases, it is also possible to free a dangerous patient because of a doctor's error. A psychiatrist may make a mistake in his or her diagnosis of a patient's condition and progress. Or, the psychiatrist may be fooled by the patient into thinking that all is well again.

Such mistakes are an admitted danger in psychiatric treatment—and for good reason. Much physical illness can be diagnosed with relative ease by observing symptoms and using such modern procedures as X rays, electrocardiograms, and various laboratory tests. But mental illness is quite another matter. Even with extensive training and experience, and even with such aids as brain scans, it is often extremely difficult to assess many mental disorders and the degree to which they are present. The diagnosis, the direction that treatment will take, and the evaluation of a patient's progress toward recovery depend on the observation of the patient's behavior, emotions, and outlook by psychiatrists. The chance of mistakenly thinking a patient totally or partially well again—and then advising a tragic early release—is always present and seemingly great.

The possibility of mistaken diagnosis and the subsequent mishandling of a patient were issues discussed during the Hinckley trial. The trial revealed that Hinckley had been at home and under the care of a psychiatrist during the year before shooting the president. The psychiatrist had advised meditation exercises for the young man and further advised that Hinckley's mental state would be helped if he were made to leave home and live on his own. This latter suggestion frightened Hinckley's brother and sister. They felt he could not handle the problems of the outside world by himself and said that he should be placed in a mental hospital for treatment. In light of what happened on March 30, 1981, they were right and the psychiatrist was tragically wrong.

Further, the psychiatrist—and another doctor who had cared for Hinckley earlier—treated him with the drug Valium. The use of Valium with schizophrenics— which Hinckley, remember, was generally diagnosed as being—is widely considered by the medical profession to be a poor choice because it may not calm the patient but instead trigger violent behavior. Hinckley himself admitted to taking twenty milligrams of Valium just before shooting President Reagan. This is two to four times the normal dosage.

In his *Reader's Digest* article, Senator Orrin Hatch points to what he regards as a special danger in the area of mistaken diagnosis. He claims that many defendants,

Garrett Trapnell was sentenced
to prison for skyjacking.

BERNE PUBLIC LIBRARY

seeing the advantages of the insanity plea, have learned to pretend to be insane. To back up his claim, he points to a study made recently at the hospital in which Hinckley is confined. The study concluded that more than 100 offenders who had been judged not guilty by reason of insanity and who were then housed at St. Elizabeths were not insane at all. They were, rather, "highly clever and manipulative" people.

Senator Hatch further backs up his claim by turning to the case of Garrett Trapnell. The senator writes that, on being arrested at age twenty for armed robbery, Trapnell learned from his lawyer that he could either go to prison for twenty years or be assigned to a state hospital. Feigning insanity, Trapnell was diagnosed as suffering from chronic paranoid schizophrenia and was placed in a Maryland mental hospital. A year later, he was judged well again and was released. His partner in the armed robbery received a lengthy prison sentence.

Trapnell went on to commit a number of armed robberies. Whenever he was arrested, he managed to convince psychiatrists that he was unbalanced. He was repeatedly confined to hospitals and then won early releases because he seemed to recover. Later, in a taped interview with a magazine writer, he said that, to pull off his feigned insanity, he had read more books on psychology and psychiatry than any student in the world.

The taped interview eventually proved to be Trapnell's undoing. When he was later arrested for skyjacking an airliner and again turned to the insanity defense, the tape was played during his trial. He was at last sent to prison.

THE EVIDENCE IS CONFUSING

When a defendant pleads not guilty by reason of insanity, much of the trial is devoted to testimony presented

[51]

by psychiatrists. They are brought to the witness stand by both the prosecution and the defense. Just how much time is given to this psychiatric evidence can be seen in the Hinckley trial. Of the forty-one witnesses who participated, eighteen were medical people. Fewer than half the witnesses, their testimony nevertheless took up two-thirds of the trial.

The opponents of the plea do not complain about the amount of time needed for the psychiatric testimony. Rather, they are concerned about two other points. First, the testimony is of a highly technical nature. Second, it presents conflicting views on the medical problems involved, with each side often reaching the exactly opposite conclusions on the very same matter. The opponents of the plea contend that these two points make it terribly difficult, if not downright impossible at times, for the jury to reach a sound verdict. Because the average juror is not trained in medicine, the testimony is often far too technical for him or her to comprehend fully. The conflicting views of the witnesses, all of them seeming to be medical experts, can further confuse matters. (Conflicting testimony, other than medical, can also lead to confusion and is inherent in many different types of trials.) The verdict, then, runs the risk of being based on guesswork rather than on an actual understanding of the issues at hand.

Again, the Hinckley trial can be used for illustration. It shows clearly the kinds of bewildering testimony that jurors can face. For example, Hinckley's medical witnesses introduced evidence to indicate that abnormalities were present in the young man's brain. The evidence centered about what is known as a CAT scan, a three-dimensional, computerized X ray made of Hinckley's brain. According to the defense witnesses, the scan revealed that certain folds in Hinckley's brain were atrophying—decaying—and thus indicated that he was incapable of rational thought at the time of the shooting. The prosecution responded by bringing in a doctor who said that he had looked at the scan and had found no indication of abnormality in the brain. Which "expert" were the jurors to believe?

In the matter of the CAT scan, the Hinckley jurors were up against yet another problem. Suppose that there had been no argument about the reading of the scan. Suppose that both the prosecution and the defense psychiatrists had agreed that it had, indeed, revealed abnormalities. Even then, the scan would not have proved conclusively that Hinckley was insane enough to be acquitted. Why? Because atrophy in certain folds on the brain show itself in normal people. It is found in 3 percent of normal people. Nor is it found in all people who are schizophrenics, but only in about 30 percent of them. Did Hinckley fall within the 3 percent of normal people or within the 30 percent of schizophrenics? Who of the jurors could tell?

But the CAT scan was only one problem encountered by Hinckley's jurors. Throughout the trial, they ran into other conflicting testimony. The defense psychiatrists spoke of Hinckley's strange background and the mistakes made by the two doctors who had treated him over the years, mistakes that, perhaps as the prescribing of Valium had done, might have worsened his mental condition. Also introduced was the fact that Hinckley had tried twice to commit suicide in the months following the attack on President Reagan. In May 1981 he swallowed a great number of sleeping pills; later in the year, after jamming his cell door with a cracker box so that the jail guards could not rush in and rescue him, he hanged himself from the cell's window bars; they cut him down as he was turning blue. All these facts pointed to a sadly unbalanced personality, but the prosecution witnesses claimed that he was well enough to have known he was committing a crime that afternoon of March 30, 1981. One doctor told the jury that Hinckley was calm and acting sensibly when he was arrested and taken to police headquarters.

And so the questions remained. What were the jurors to believe? Who was telling the truth? How were they, as non-medical people, to evaluate all that they heard and then make a sound and reasonable decision?

In addition to confusing the jurors, it has been argued that the conflicting psychiatric evidence tilted the case too much in Hinckley's favor. With the trial held in federal court, the prosecution bore the burden of proof and so had to establish Hinckley's sanity beyond a reasonable doubt. Because the testimony was so technical, so difficult to understand, and so contradictory, the shadow of doubt thus created left jurors no alternative but to decide on a not-guilty verdict.

A WORRY ABOUT FAIRNESS

The opponents of the plea are not only worried about the confusions created by the medical testimony. They are also gravely concerned that much of it is not objective, unbiased fact because psychiatrists are hired by one side or the other to appear as witnesses, and then are paid by that side for their courtroom appearances. Consequently, it is sometimes suspected that some psychiatrists may slant their testimony in favor of their side.

In the minds of many people, slanted testimony—a danger in any trial—is especially easy to come by in insanity cases. Psychiatry, remember, is not yet (and may never be) the exact science that other branches of medicine are. Diagnosis is very much a matter of opinion on the part of the psychiatrists. Great, then, is the risk for slanted opinions, either unfairly or at times downright dishonestly stated, to substantiate the position of their side.

Certainly this does not apply to all psychiatrists. There are countless medical people who have too much integrity to slant their testimony. But it is a well-known fact that there are some who make a profitable "business" or "profession" of testifying in court and angling their evidence in favor of whichever side hires them. They appear in case after case. They are known contemptuously to their fellow physicians and even to the attorneys who hire them as "professional witnesses."

Law professor Stephen Cohen of the Georgetown University Law Center at Washington, D.C., echoes this contempt in his article on the Hinckley case, "It's a Mad, Mad Verdict," which appeared in the July 12, 1982, issue of *The New Republic*. He indicates that professional witnesses may not be very knowledgeable or competent doctors to begin with because, making a career for themselves in court, they engage in little outside medical practice.

He cites a statement by Dr. Willard Gaylin, a distinguished authority of law and psychiatry. Dr. Gaylin has said that, if you were to list the names of 50 to 10,000 of the leading psychiatrists, you would not find on it any of the doctors who are professional witnesses.

Attorneys have often been criticized for hiring witnesses who are willing to slant their testimony and thus turn a trial into a "game." The attorneys reply that it is their responsibility to build the strongest case possible for their side, but that they're forced to work with the tools at hand. They'd like to use the best doctors but often find them too busy with their own patients to take the time for a court appearance. Many doctors are afraid that a court appearance will damage their reputations, that they will be accused of joining the ranks of the professionals. The attorneys say that they hope a professional witness will, indeed, come up with legitimate testimony but are fully aware that he or she will bend things as needs be.

In addition to the risk of slanted—or even dishonest—testimony, the opponents of the plea see yet another problem in the use of professional witnesses. In time, these witnesses become accustomed to working in court. They no longer are as nervous as people who take the witness stand for the first time. This very natural and expected nervousness often experienced by first-time witnesses can—and sometimes does—damage their testimony by making them fidget, stammer, hesitate, and even express things the wrong way. The professionals become, as a West Coast attorney says, "really slick," giving their testimony in a polished and confident manner that "makes them look as if they really know what they're talking about."

Obviously, the danger seen here is that the polished performance—and not the true medical abilities of the witness or the substance of the testimony being given—will be what impresses some or all of the jurors and leads to a mistaken verdict.

The same situation may well apply when professional witnesses are pitted against each other. One may have some solid evidence to give. But, even though accustomed to appearing in court, he or she may not be as polished as an opposition witness who has material of less substance to offer. Again, there is the great danger that at least some of the jurors will be impressed for the wrong reasons.

It must be said, however, that trials don't always work out this way. Professor Stephen Cohen, in his article for *The New Republic,* writes that the defense attorneys in the Hinckley trial did not turn to professionals for all of their witnesses. Rather, they brought to the stand two distinguished psychiatrists, both of whom are respected researchers in schizophrenia, Drs. William Carpenter and Michael Bear. Neither man had ever before testified in court. Professor Cohen reports that both seemed ill at ease while on the stand. But, regardless of their nervousness, their testimony obviously impressed the jurors, as was shown by the final verdict.

A RICH MAN'S DEFENSE

Much of the public anger over the Hinckley verdict can be traced to the fact that the young man came from a wealthy family.

The press reported that his parents had been able to afford one of the best and highest-priced law firms in Washington, D.C., and had been able to pay for the services of such highly respected psychiatric witnesses as Drs. Carpenter and Bear. In all, Hinckley's parents were reported to have spent an estimated half million dollars on their son's defense.

Because of what the Hinckleys were able to do, many people regard the insanity plea as grossly unfair. They argue that it must be dropped or changed because it favors only those defendants wealthy enough to hire the very best and most expensive legal and psychiatric talent. Defendants unable to afford such help are put at an extreme disadvantage and run a far greater risk of punishment than do wealthy defendants. (This inequality is not just limited to insanity pleas.) All this, the opponents argue, constitutes a violation of the basic concept that all people, regardless of wealth or social position, should be given equal treatment at the hands of the law.

Among those angered by the Hinckley verdict was Republican Senator Larry Pressler of South Dakota. He told the press: "The insanity plea is a rich man's defense. A poor man can use it successfully only if he is a *cause célèbre* [someone whose case has attracted widespread public attention] or [if] somebody else finances it."

Republican Senator Larry Pressler argues that the insanity plea favors the wealthy.

The people who favor keeping the insanity plea are forced to admit that Senator Pressler has a point. Many of them agree that there seems little doubt that the plea does favor the wealthy. But they point out that Hinckley's wealth very likely had no real effect on the final verdict; remember, as stated earlier, the jury was left with a serious doubt about Hinckley's sanity and so had little choice but to declare him not guilty. But we will further examine their views in the next chapter.

And now, having looked at the principal arguments presented by those who wish to see the plea dropped or changed, we come to the opposite viewpoint. What is being said by the people who favor the plea and want to see it left as it is?

5

For
the
Plea

"Fairness" is the word that sums up the most basic argument offered by the many people who believe that the plea should be left as is or should, if altered, be changed but slightly. They feel it only fair for the law to give special consideration to unbalanced defendants, especially those who are severely affected. The deranged, as are the mentally defective, are the helpless victims of a disease or accident. They can no more be blamed for their condition than can someone be blamed for having measles. Nor can they be any more blamed for their offenses than can the patient who accidentally knocks over a bedside lamp while tossing restlessly in the grip of a raging fever. It is unjust to punish them.

Pursuing the idea of fairness, the supporters of the plea quickly point out that sane defendants receive special considerations. For instance, adults are often given lighter sentences for first-time offenses than for second- and third-time ones; convicts have the chance to win parole from prison for good behavior. Special consideration, of course, goes to very young children. And every effort is made to rehabilitate older juveniles as well. In addition, their cases are heard in special courts and their slates are wiped clean when they reach adulthood; all this is done with the aim of eventually turning them into law-abiding and useful adults rather than criminals.

Since help is provided in all these instances, why should the insane be excluded from extra consideration? They should have the opportunity to argue that they were so ill at the time of their offenses as to be held blameless and then, if their condition still warrants it, to be placed in an institution designed to help them rather than in a prison where a lesser degree of assistance—or no help at all—would be available.

Supporters of the plea recognize that some defendants do abuse it, turning to it without justification and then escaping punishment. But, the supporters argue, a number of sane convicts break the law when they are released on parole, yet there is no great public demand to dismantle the entire parole system. A dismantling is seen as unfair because it would cause suffering for all those men and women who do not violate their paroles. Despite the way it is sometimes misused, the parole system is widely held as valuable in that it gives many deserving convicts an early chance to start life afresh; to dismantle it because of trouble now and again would be akin to the old saying of "throwing out the baby with the bath water." The very same applies to the insanity plea. It is unjust to call for an end to the plea, a thing of value to all the mentally helpless, simply because it is violated on occasion.

The supporters also argue that the plea is among the many civil rights safeguards that protect the accused against public and governmental vindictiveness. Other laws protect sane defendants against being quickly and angrily punished for anything from a crime to an antigovernment political stance. The plea performs the same service for the insane defendant, especially the offender who arouses widespread outrage, as did Hinckley, by attacking a well-known figure. Such an attack is terrible, yes. But the punishment of the deranged offender out of a sense of public or governmental wrath or revenge would be just as terrible, if not more so. It would add up to a national lynching.

Congressman Thomas P. "Tip" O'Neill (Democrat, Massachusetts), the Speaker of the House of Representatives, commented on this point in the wake of the attack on President Reagan. Calling the U.S. legal system "the fairest in the world," O'Neill told the press that in some countries "Hinckley would have been dead and buried in eight days, but we don't work that way."

A JUST DEFENSE

Its supporters, then, see the plea as both just and valuable. They add that its justice and value are recognized internationally. It has long been found, in one form or another, in virtually every civilized nation. Such would not be the case if it were without substance. To dispense with the plea or to alter it drastically would be to ignore a value that nations across the world have found essential over the centuries.

Further, in the eyes of many legal experts, no just purpose would be achieved by dropping or significantly altering the plea. Judge Irving R. Kaufman of the United States Court of Appeals summed up what is meant here in an article that he wrote for the August 8, 1982, edition of *The New York Times*. The article was titled "The Insanity Plea on Trial."

In it, Judge Kaufman explains that legal scholars over the years have come to see criminal justice as having four basic aims: (1) the rehabilitation of the guilty, (2) the deterrence of future offenses, (3) the protection of

**U.S. Court of Appeals Judge Irving Kaufman
supports the insanity plea.**

the public from dangerous individuals, and (4) retribution or, as Judge Kaufman prefers to call it, punishment that is just. He then writes that the idea of dropping or drastically revising the plea goes against these four purposes.

To begin, there will be little or no chance to rehabilitate insane defendants if they are sent to prisons rather than to mental institutions where they can be more adequately treated. Nor will the punishing of the insane deter them from future offenses, neither while in prison nor after their release. Their very mental unbalance makes them, to use Judge Kaufman's word, "undeterrable." The judge's point here is that the only way to deter future offenses is to attempt to cure the insane to the point where they are no longer dangerous. Further, the imprisonment of an insane defendant will not stop other deranged people from committing crimes. They haven't the wit to stop and think twice out of the fear that they may receive the same punishment. They, too, cannot be deterred.

A prison sentence may well protect the public from a dangerously insane individual, but the same protection is to be had by confining the defendant for care in a mental institution. In fact, as many plea supporters see it, confinement for care provides an even greater protection. For now the defendant is given the help that might well lead to a point of recovery that no longer leaves him or her a danger to self or society.

Finally, Judge Kaufman does not see punishment of the insane as a just punishment. How can the punishment of people who do not know what they're doing ever be just? Along with others who have looked into the legal problems surrounding insanity, the judge believes that, too often, the imprisoning of the insane offender adds up to the public revenge mentioned earlier. He quotes the noted sixteenth-century British philosopher and author Sir Francis Bacon. Bacon called revenge "a kind of wild justice which the more man's nature runs to it, the more ought the law weed it out."

NOT WIDELY USED

The several views mentioned thus far have been general and basic. Now we come to points that are more specific. In the main, these points are replies given by the plea supporters to opinions expressed by the opponents.

A principal anti-plea argument, of course, is that it can be widely used by sane or somewhat unbalanced offenders to escape a deserved punishment. The supporters answer that the plea is not as widely used as its opponents would have everyone believe. To substantiate this view, they turn to a number of national and state statistics.

There are no figures to show exactly how often the plea is attempted throughout the United States. However, estimates by legal and medical experts hold that it is used in less than 1 percent of all the nation's criminal cases. Out of what must certainly be thousands of cases, there are only about 1,600 acquittals each year on the grounds of insanity.

Statistics from the individual states are somewhat more exact. In New York State, for instance, the plea is attempted in only 1.5 percent of the several thousand criminal cases up for trial annually.

NOT A CONVENIENT
LOOPHOLE

What of the anti-plea claim that it can be used as a convenient loophole to escape a deserved punishment? Not really true, reply the supporters. While admitting that the genuinely guilty have occasionally won with the plea, they argue that its use involves four difficulties that make it anything but an escape hatch.

The first—and undoubtedly the greatest—difficulty

centers on the very nature of an insanity trial. In other criminal trials, the accused is presumed innocent by everyone until proven guilty. But, when the plea is used, the defendant, remember, admits to committing the offense and then asks that certain circumstances be considered to find him or her innocent. The jurors know that they are dealing with an admitted offender and their minds, perhaps never to change, can be easily set in favor of a guilty verdict right from the start.

Second, it is a well-established fact that jurors are not willing to acquit someone on the grounds of insanity unless the insanity is obvious and extreme or the evidence in support of it is very strong. Along with everyone else, the jurors are fully aware that insanity can be used as a convenient excuse or can be expertly feigned. They're on the lookout for these two problems and can be unremittingly suspicious of any claim that they are not present in the case.

Third, it's another well-known fact that jurors are reluctant to find a defendant not guilty when they know—as do most people today—that their verdict may well lead to a later unwise release from confinement for care. They do not want it on their conscience that their decision eventually ended in a release that saw the defendant commit new acts of violence.

Finally, in widely publicized and much discussed cases such as John Hinckley's, the jurors cannot help but be aware of the public anger directed toward the defendant. They themselves may share that anger. Before they can reach an unbiased decision, they face the enormous task of putting aside their own feelings and the worry of what the public will say of them should they reach a not-guilty verdict. It's a job that some jurors may not be able to do successfully.

In addition to these four factors, the supporters turn to a set of statistics for proof of their point. The statistics show not only that the plea is used in a small percentage of trials but that it also has a high failure rate. On both the federal and state levels, it fails to bring in a not-guilty verdict in about three out of every four cases.

Faced as it is with a quartet of difficulties and with such a failure rate, the supporters flatly state that it is unreasonable to label the plea a convenient loophole to avoid punishment.

THE PROBLEM OF
PSYCHIATRIC EVIDENCE

Now we come to the reply given to the anti-plea argument that the psychiatric testimony leads to mistaken verdicts because it is so technical, so conflicting, and so often slanted by professional witnesses in favor of the side that has hired them.

The supporters hold that the average juror is an intelligent person. Though not a medical expert and though some of what is said may well be beyond the grasp of any lay person, he or she certainly has the brains to follow, comprehend, and then decide on most testimony of a technical nature. To think otherwise is simply to take the snobbish view that all people are too stupid to fathom problems of any complication. Further, before going off to consider their verdict, all juries receive instructions from the judge as to the legal problems and requirements they must face in reaching a final decision. These instructions can often help to clarify for them certain confusing items of testimony.

These very same points also apply to conflicting evidence. The supporters believe that the great majority of jurors have the insight and the common sense to help them decide who is giving the most valid testimony.

On top of all else, as Judge Irving Kaufman remarks in his *New York Times* article, it is a well-known fact in courts that jurors, when faced with testimony that has become too tangled and technical, will turn to their own experiences in life and their own common sense to arrive at a verdict. They have, as often as not, reached very appropriate decisions.

It should also be remembered, the supporters argue, that jurors must consider technical testimony in trials other than insanity cases—testimony concerning such varied matters as engineering, automotive design, weather conditions, science, and physical medicine. The testimony here can be as confusing and as contradictory as that found in an insanity trial. No one criticizes the use of such testimony or calls for changes in the law because of the difficulties it presents. Such testimony is seen as a necessary part of trying these cases. Why, then, single out the insanity plea alone for change because of the confusing testimony that can rise out of it?

As to the charge that the testimony can be slanted, the supporters acknowledge that it often is. But, they quickly add, this is not the fault of the plea itself. It's the fault of those witnesses who can be "bought" by one side or the other. This situation is not to be corrected by taking action against the plea. Instead, the corrective steps should be directed against the professional witnesses. Several basic recommendations for controlling psychiatric testimony are now being widely discussed. We'll come to them in the next chapter.

Nor, the supporters point out, are insanity trials the only ones stained with slanted testimony. Experts who are willing to go to court for a price are, like technical testimony itself, just as likely to be found in other trials. Recently, the press reported that so many experts are becoming available for hire as professional witnesses that companies have been formed to put them in touch with attorneys needing their services. The companies either provide appropriate witnesses from names in their files or go in search of the exact sort of witness needed for a particular case. A fee is charged to the attorney for the company's work. It is said to range somewhere between $120 and $250 per witness.

So the question remains. Why attack the insanity plea alone? It's the *whole* problem of professional witnesses that needs to be cleared up.

Finally, the supporters argue that some states have already taken steps against the confusions of psychiatric testimony and the possibility that some of it will be slanted. These states do not depend solely on the testimony of psychiatrists hired by the opposing sides. Rather, they require that all defendants attempting the insanity plea be examined by state psychiatrists. As employees of the state, such psychiatrists are not paid for their courtroom appearances and so have nothing to gain by bending their testimony in one direction or another.

Michigan is among the states following this practice. Each year, about 1,400 defendants seek to use the insanity plea in Michigan. They are all examined by state psychiatrists. Of the 1,400, the psychiatrists usually support the insanity claims of fewer than 100 defendants. The psychiatrists then take their findings to court and appear in addition to the prosecution and defense witnesses. It has been found that juries usually go along with their findings—either for or against the defendant—and render their verdicts accordingly. In all, this control over the plea itself and over the testimony enables only a small percentage—less than 10 percent— of all the plea attempts to end successfully for the defendant.

THE PROBLEM OF
UNWISE RELEASE

Again, the supporters must admit that another anti-plea complaint has some merit. Press reports of such men as robber and skyjacker Garrett Trapnell and Hawaii's

Robert E. Miller leave no doubt that some defendants acquitted for insanity have been later unwisely released from confinement for care. Adding to this certainty is the story of George Fitzsimmons, who was judged innocent by reason of insanity for the murder of his parents some years ago. Sent to a mental hospital, he eventually convinced the doctors that he was no longer dangerous and was released so that he could live with his aunt and uncle. Though he told the hospital staff that he dearly loved the two relatives, Fitzsimmons stabbed them to death soon after entering their home.

The Trapnell, Miller, and Fitzsimmons cases—and all like them—are tragic. But, again, the supporters maintain that the problem here, as in other instances, does not lie with the plea itself.

It lies, rather, with all the various factors that are making unwise releases increasingly possible. It lies, in some states, with laws that permit hospitals to release an unbalanced patient on their own authority. It lies, in other states, with laws that can jam already-crowded court calendars with required hearings on patient complaints and petitions for release. It lies with those mental care workers who, in their enthusiasm for the idea of rehabilitation, think that a patient is rehabilitated to the point of no longer being dangerous when such is not the case. It lies with psychiatrists and psychologists who can make the all-too-human error of wrongly diagnosing a patient's improvement or of being fooled by the patient. It lies with the use of psychotropic drugs that can put the symptoms of a mental illness into remission and cause the patient to act normally—but only for as long as the drugs are used.

These problems, the supporters contend, will not be solved by attacking the plea. The problems themselves must be solved. But—and here many supporters and opponents are in agreement—some of the problems surrounding unwise releases may well be beyond a completely satisfactory solution. What can be done legally to ease the burden on court calendars when the civil rights of individuals demand that their petitions for release and their complaints be heard? What can be done to guarantee that no staff member in a mental institution will ever again recommend a patient's release through error or the enthusiastic hope that all is well again? And what can be done to keep a patient, appearing normal because of a psychotropic drug, from stopping the medication when released and reverting to his or her former dangerous behavior?

On the surface at least, there seems to be but one sure-fire answer to these puzzles: hold all the acquitted defendants in confinement for care for the rest of their lives. But both the plea supporters and many of its opponents quickly reply that such a practice would be grossly unfair—and a violation of civil rights—in cases where release is actually justified. One such case was that of an Oregon woman who was mentioned in the 1983 NBC television program on insanity and the law. Some time ago, following teen years marked by mental problems, she, without warning, killed her parents with a rifle. Found not guilty due to insanity, she was confined to a mental hospital. Since then, her condition has so improved that she has been released from the hospital on an out-patient basis. She is now living in an apartment of her own and, receiving out-patient care five days a week, seems to be moving successfully toward a normal and even productive life.

The supporters additionally argue that, should the plea be altered or dropped altogether, all the above problems will not go away. Suppose the plea is dropped and insane defendants are sent to prison, perhaps to receive psychiatric care while there, perhaps not. What will happen once they've served their sentences and

This photo, a self-portrait of John Hinckley,
was used as evidence in his trial.

have thus paid their debt to society? Depending on the laws of the area in which they are imprisoned, their release may be required even if they are mentally incompetent or they may be confined for further care if judged still too hazardous to themselves and society. And so the problems take shape again. Potentially dangerous prisoners can be turned loose as soon as they have served their sentences. If there is further confinement, there can be those periodic petitions for release. There can be mistaken diagnoses as to the degree of recovery. There can be patients who fool the doctor. In a word, nothing has changed.

Though there seems to be but one sure-fire—and totally unacceptable—solution to all the problems, it must be said that one state, Oregon, has put a unique method into effect for handling mental defendants confined for care. It is proving to be successful and may provide a major solution to the problems. We'll talk in Chapter Seven of what Oregon is doing.

A RICH MAN'S DEFENSE

And still again, the plea supporters must agree that yet another of the opponents' complaints has merit—that the insanity plea is a "rich man's defense." The plea, you'll remember, is widely accused of denying equal protection under the law to everyone by being of advantage mainly to those defendants who can afford the costs of a high-quality defense team and the services of expensive psychiatric witnesses, or who have friends or relatives with ample money to foot the bill for them. At the core of this argument is the fact that Hinckley's parents were able to spend an estimated $500,000 on their son's defense. It's the fact that caused Senator Larry Pressler to remark in the wake of the Hinckley trial that a poor defendant can use the plea successfully "only if he is a *cause célèbre* or [if] somebody else finances it."

The plea supporters, you'll recall from Chapter Four, reply to this argument by saying that Hinckley's family wealth had nothing to do with the outcome of his case because the verdict was reached on the grounds that the prosecution failed to provide convincing proof that he was sane on that March day in 1981. They further counter the complaint with the view that the poor defendant who pleads insanity may well become a *cause célèbre,* gaining much attention in the press because of the plea itself or because of the violent nature of the crime committed. As a result, he or she is almost certain to attract a high-priced attorney who is drawn to the case because of its challenge or publicity value. The help given here will be without charge or will be priced within the defendant's means. The supporters then add that defendants who are too poor to afford legal representation are assigned public defenders, whose salaries are paid by public monies. Though public defenders are not as highly reimbursed as were Hinckley's attorneys, they are nonetheless capable of adequately representing and protecting the defendant in court.

We've now discussed the opposing views in the debate over the insanity plea. Two more steps remain in completing the picture of the debate. First, we must look at what actually *can* be done to settle the debate. Then we must turn to what *is* being done.

6

What Can Be Done?

This chapter will deal mainly with views of the plea opponents because they are the people who want to eliminate or significantly change the insanity plea. But the supporters who want to retain the plea as it is won't go ignored. Throughout the chapter, we'll be talking about their reactions to the various ideas being proposed.

One point about the views of many opponents must be made clear right at the start. While they hope to see the plea abolished or revised, they have no wish to go so far as to give *no* consideration at all to mentally disturbed defendants. They realize that no consideration whatsoever would be unfair, particularly to those defendants who are extremely disturbed. They acknowledge that many defendants deserve to be given psychiatric help and not to be simply locked away in a cell. Not to give such help would be as heartless as not providing medical care for prisoners suffering physical ills such as cancer and diabetes. But they also believe that, in the name of justice, something must be done to keep offenders who are unbalanced to a lesser degree and those who are quite sane from using the plea as a convenient technicality to avoid punishment.

As a result of these views, many opponents do not want to see the insanity plea abolished or changed without substituting measures that would continue to give reasonable consideration to the extremely insane. They have, in the main, then, come up with a number of measures that can be called compromises because they attempt to strike a balance between the needs of the defendants and the need that justice be done. The first compromise measure calls for a new verdict to be added to insanity trials.

A NEW VERDICT

As is true in all criminal cases, the jurors in an insanity trial can arrive at one of only two verdicts—guilty or not guilty. These verdicts work fine in other trials, but they create a problem in insanity cases.

This is because they force the jury to two extremes. Either the jurors must find the defendant sane enough for conviction or deranged enough for acquittal. There is no in-between area. But mental illnesses have an "in-between" area because they affect their victims in varying degrees and in varying ways. And so what are the jurors to do when, as so often happens, they're faced with an "in-between" defendant—the individual who is markedly ill but not ill enough to meet the legal requirements for a not-guilty decision. You'll remember from Chapter Three that those requirements, as set forth in the ALI rule, call for defendants to be so ill as not to have understood the nature of their offense, or so ill as to have been unable to conform their conduct to the demands of the law.

The proposed new verdict is meant to take care of any such problem as this. Were you the defendant, it

John Hinckley, in police custody, leaving
U.S. District Court after his arraignment

would enable the jurors to declare you *guilty but mentally unbalanced*. The verdict, which is sometimes also called *guilty but insane*, would hold you to have been reasonable enough in your mind at the time of the offense to be held responsible for it and thus to be deserving of punishment. But with the verdict, the jurors would also recognize that you are sufficiently ill to require psychiatric care.

The verdict would see four things happen to you. First, just as if you were a convicted sane defendant, you would receive a prison sentence. Second, you would be examined by psychiatrists. Next, were they to find you sufficiently well again, you would immediately be sent to prison; if found still unwell, you would be assigned to a mental facility for treatment. Finally, should you recover before finishing your sentence, you would be discharged from the facility and made to serve the remainder of your prison term. Should you not recover, however, the facility could hold you for treatment as long as necessary, even beyond the length of your sentence.

Proponents of this approach say that the guilty-but-mentally-ill verdict can accomplish several ends. It can acknowledge your legal guilt but still provide you with needed care. Making you serve your entire sentence, it can extend the time you're kept away from the public and so can offset a danger in the present way of doing things—the risk that you'll be unwisely freed from confinement for care only to do further violence. It can well deter a number of future crimes by warning potential offenders that the claim of insanity no longer promises to be a convenient excuse to avoid punishment. And, in a time when the courts stand accused of being too lenient, it can show everyone that the law recognizes your crime, even though committed when you were unbalanced, to have nevertheless been a serious offense against society and is doing something about it.

Though liked by many people, the proposed new verdict has drawn much criticism. A chief objection centers on the possibility of jury error. Should a jury mistakenly underestimate a defendant's condition, a person who is genuinely not responsible for his or her offense could be punished in the same way as a responsible individual. This goes against the long-standing legal principal that it is unjust to treat the responsible and the not-responsible as one and the same.

Another widespread complaint is that the verdict is both cruel and fruitless. John Hinckley's parents—Jack and Jo Ann Hinckley—stressed this point in the article "Insanity Is the Culprit," which they wrote for the March 1983 issue of *Reader's Digest*. They called the verdict cruel because it threatens to punish so many mentally helpless individuals. And fruitless because it will deter neither the convicted defendants themselves nor unbalanced would-be offenders from future acts of violence. Here they are echoing the sentiments of Judge Irving R. Kaufman who, as was reported in Chapter Five, has called all such people "undeterrable" by virtue of their mental conditions. Echoing Judge Kaufman on another anticipated problem, the Hinckleys feel that the new verdict will make it easy to punish defendants out of a sense of public wrath or revenge.

The Hinckleys, along with many other critics of the verdict, also look on it as meting out a "double punishment." Defendants who should have been found legally innocent of their offenses in the first place will not only be held in confinement for care for perhaps a long period but will then, when others would be freed on being judged well again, be made to spend additional time in prison. John Hinckley himself, in a statement written in St. Elizabeths Hospital and then published on Septem-

An undated photo of John Hinckley
in front of the White House

ber 20, 1982 by *Newsweek*, sees another danger in this "double punishment." It is the possibility that, on being dispatched to prison, a recovered individual will fall ill again because of the harsh conditions there. Hinckley accuses prisons of not rehabilitating people but of fostering unbalanced and antisocial behavior. Both he and his parents argue that there is only one reasonable way to handle the insane, and that is to care for and rehabilitate them, not punish them.

CONTROLLING
PSYCHIATRIC TESTIMONY

A number of proposals for changing the insanity plea center on psychiatric testimony, which is often highly technical, conflicting, and slanted.

One proposal has to do with the psychiatrists and psychologists who appear as witnesses. Basically, two kinds of witnesses participate in trials: ordinary witnesses and expert witnesses. Ordinary witnesses are permitted to testify on only those matters that they personally know to be factual; they may, for instance, speak only of what they actually saw of a crime or what they actually heard said by the people involved in it; they may not say what they heard someone else remark or gossip about the crime, nor may they—and this is the important point here—give their own opinions about anything concerning the crime or the defendant. Expert witnesses, on the other hand, can both testify as to what they personally know to be the facts of the case and also, because of their expertise in their line of work, give their opinions on certain matters pertaining to the offense and the defendant.

The medical people who appear in insanity trials do so as expert witnesses. Should you be the defendant, they can first give factual evidence; they can describe your condition and symptoms; they can speak of what they've actually observed of your behavior. But then they can go on to give their opinions of your case; they can give their opinions on the degree of your insanity at the time of the offense and on the question of whether your unbalance was such that you should be judged either guilty or innocent of the crime.

In the minds of many people, it is this opinion testimony that causes the most trouble in insanity trials. It seems to cause most of the conflicting testimony and enables some witnesses to slant their remarks. Further, even though it comes from medical personnel, much of the opinion must be looked on as questionable because the precise nature and degree of mental illnesses can be so difficult to pinpoint beyond doubt.

The recommendation here is that the testimony of the medical witnesses be curtailed and limited to facts only. The witnesses would be prohibited from giving any opinions on your condition, most especially on the question of whether your insanity was such as to find you guilty or not guilty. The jurors would have to determine such matters for themselves on the basis of the medical facts presented.

The proposal has long been discussed and supported by many legal experts. Recently, a special study group was formed by the American Bar Association to look into the problems of the insanity plea. The group recommended that the insanity plea be retained as it is and that the proposed curtailment of opinion testimony be put into effect.

Among those who like the proposal are a number of leading psychiatrists and psychologists. As medically trained personnel, they say that they are able to give the facts of a defendant's illness and behavior. But, despite their medical training, they do not feel in a position to give opinions on whether the defendant meets the legal requirements to be judged guilty or innocent. Though they may have their own private views of what the verdict should be, they see the judging of those requirements to be a legal and not a medical matter. Thus, it should be left with the court and the jury. The psychiatrists and psychologists also say that giving opinions often forces them—in a trial itself and especially in later hearings to consider petitions for release from care—into the position of predicting the defendant's future condition and behavior. This is an impossible position to be in. They know that, even though medically trained, they are no more able to predict the future than is anyone else.

BALANCING THE TESTIMONY

As yet another solution to the testimony problem, it has been recommended that the approach used by several states, among them Michigan, be followed nationwide. These are the states that do not depend solely on the testimony of the witnesses hired by either side. Each defendant planning to use the plea in Michigan, you'll recall from Chapter Five, is examined by state psychiatrists. Their testimony, presumed to be unbiased because they represent neither side, is presented in addition to that of the prosecution and defense witnesses. It is a practice that, in the eyes of many, gives a balance to all the testimony and offsets the influence of testimony that might be slanted.

ANOTHER BALANCE

A similar proposal calls for the court to appoint an independent panel of psychiatrists and psychologists before each insanity trial. Their job would be to appear not on behalf of either the prosecution or the defense but on behalf of the court itself. The panel members would examine the defendant. They would give testimony as to his or her condition. They would explain to the jurors any points difficult to understand in the testimony presented by the prosecution and defense witnesses. They would help the jury evaluate all the medical testimony.

And they would assist the judge in preparing information needed by the jury and others on certain medical-legal points.

In total, as in the Michigan practice, there would be a balancing of the testimony and less of an opportunity for slanted testimony. And, as important, the proposal would enable jurors to have highly technical and confusing points of evidence explained to them by unbiased participants in the trial.

Several difficulties, however, are seen in the use of such a panel. Judge Irving R. Kaufman speaks of them in his *New York Times* article. He comments that, first, great care must be taken by the court to ensure that the panel members remain impartial because there is always the risk that they may become influenced in favor of one side or the other. Second, the court must likewise take great care that the jury does not begin to regard the panel members as being infallible, incapable of making a mistake, just because they happen to be unbiased participants in the trial; if the jurors fail to use their own intelligence in reaching a decision but simply go along blindly with the panel's testimony, they won't be giving the defendant a fair trial. Finally, there is the possibility in some cases that the whole purpose of the panel system will backfire—that the jurors may become even more confused when the panel's technical testimony is added to that of the prosecution and the defense.

SHIFT THE BURDEN OF PROOF

As was explained in Chapter Three, the prosecution must carry the burden of proof in insanity cases being tried under federal law and must convince a jury beyond a reasonable doubt that the defendant was sufficiently sane enough at the time of the offense to be convicted. State laws vary on the burden of proof, with some states requiring the prosecution to bear it, while others place it with the defense. In the latter case, the defense attorneys are required to show that the main weight of the trial evidence—the preponderance of the evidence—indicates that the severity of the mental illness of the defendant was sufficient to bring in a verdict of not guilty.

Many plea opponents urge that the burden of proof be placed at *all* times with the defense. Their logic here is simple. As the defendant, you're making a special claim to be found innocent of an offense that you've admitted committing. Having made that claim, it's unreasonable for you to sit back and force the other side to prove you wrong or a liar. It should be your duty to justify the claim. Otherwise, you are given an advantage that tips everything unfairly in your favor.

As the plea opponents see it, a shift of the burden of proof to the defense would balance the scales of justice. Undeserving defendants would find it more difficult to use the plea successfully. Extremely deranged defendants, by virtue of the obvious seriousness of their conditions, would have every chance of benefiting from it.

But there is a question of whether it is legally possible to make such a shift.

The problem here stems in great part from a case heard by the U.S. Supreme Court in 1970. The Court decreed that, in federal trials, the prosecution must prove every element in a criminal case. As you know, a claim of insanity seeks to find the defendant innocent by removing one of the key elements in any crime— that of criminal intent. Thus, since the prosecution in a federal trial must prove *all* elements in the case, it also must be the side to prove that the defendant's insanity was insufficient to cancel the key element of criminal intent. This being so, it is impossible to transfer the burden of proof to the defense.

The problem, however, has an additional wrinkle to

it, one caused by a decision that the court reached eighteen years earlier. When considering the circumstances surrounding a 1950 question, the Court held that it can be legal to shift the burden to the defense.

And so, with two decisions that seem much at odds with each other, there is the dilemma of what is actually the legal truth of the matter. At present, as we'll see in the next chapter, the U.S. Congress is considering proposed legislation for a shift at the federal level. If enacted, the legislation not only will affect federal trials but will very likely induce a similar shift in states where the burden now lies with the prosecution. The legislation will undoubtedly have to be tested in court—including the Supreme Court—as to its legality. We may then have a final answer to a knotty question central to the future of the insanity plea.

ABOLISH THE PLEA

Opinions of what can be done to abolish the plea as it stands today take several directions. For one, some opponents feel that the job can be done simply by taking away its status as a special defense.

To understand the impact of this idea, you need only recall from Chapter Three just how important the plea as a special defense is to you, the defendant. Because of that status, you can admit to an offense and still ask to be found completely innocent of it. As in the Hinckley case, you can ask to be judged totally innocent when charged with an offense that everyone knows you committed. The dangers you'll face are obvious should that status be eliminated.

Were the plea to be demoted, it would fall under the general defense category. As an admitted or unmistakably guilty offender, you would have your insanity taken into consideration but not on today's black-and-white basis of finding you either guilty or innocent solely because of it. Your degree of insanity might be judged great enough to see you more deserving of care than punishment. It might be sufficient to see you convicted of a lesser charge and given a lighter sentence, as can happen with the general defense of diminished capacity. Or it might see you sane enough to be convicted as charged. Then, at trial's end, it would play a part in helping the court to determine what, if any, psychiatric care you now need.

The loss of the special defense status would, as many in favor of the idea see it, serve the same ends as the other moves against the plea. Undeserving defendants would be on the spot. Offenders deserving of punishment would receive it. The most severely unbalanced would receive needed help. And, with the tendency being to imprison as well as confine for care, the public would be protected from the danger of defendants being mistakenly released only to do further violence.

Other calls for abolishing the plea are directed against the current American Law Institute rule. The ALI rule was first widely adopted because of its flexibility and broadness of scope. Now, some years later, these very same factors have come under fire. The rule is being criticized in many quarters for proving so broad and flexible that it is enabling undeserving offenders to abuse it too easily. The demand is that it be sharply curtailed or dropped altogether and that it be replaced with something that provides a better method of safeguarding against abuse. The insanity plea could thus no longer be used exactly as it is today.

There is a growing feeling that all criminal courts, at both the federal and state level, should return to the M'Naghton Rule, in one form or another. It is argued that the rule, which is still followed in some states, would provide a more solid footing for judging cases than seems possible today and would certainly exercise a firmer control over defendants attempting to plead insanity. With some provision made to improve its stance on delusions, the rule would see defendants once more judged on the basic grounds of having not known what they were doing or of having not known right from wrong. Such mysterious factors as delusions, irresistible impulses, and schizophrenic fantasies leading to a loss of self-control—all so hard to judge and all so easy to claim as excuses—would no longer in themselves be the matters determining guilt or innocence. Rather, such factors would be judged against the standards set forth by the rule.

A return to the M'Naghton Rule would constitute what is called a "narrowing" of the insanity defense. Other narrowings, all intended to make the plea less advantageous for undeserving defendants, have been suggested. One advises that just one or the other of M'Naghton's two points be used and that the other be dropped. This could see defendants tried only, say, on the grounds of having not known right from wrong, while the possibility of having not known what they were doing is not even considered. Or a reverse procedure could be used. Then the defendants would be judged on whether they possessed what is called *the requisite state of mind* for their offenses. In this instance, the single question for jury consideration would be: Did the defendant know what he or she was doing at the time of the offense? If so, the verdict would have to be guilty.

But, as does a shift in the burden of proof, these various suggestions all pose a problem. They may run into trouble with the provisions in the U.S. Constitution that protect the rights of anyone accused of a crime. They may, for a number of technical reasons, keep defendants from enjoying the right to the best defense possible in the light of today's understanding of mental illness. They may, for instance, prevent defendants with certain illnesses from readily establishing that they did not have criminal intent when such a claim would be fully justified. Many legal experts believe that the suggestions could prove unconstitutional. Many others disagree. But there are no definite answers one way or the other.

Only time—should any of the suggestions be put into law and then be challenged in court—will provide the answer.

A RECENT MOVE

One of the latest moves against the insanity plea has come from the American Medical Association (AMA). During a meeting at Los Angeles in December 1983, 350 members of the AMA's policymaking body approved a resolution recommending that the plea be abolished.

Though finding the plea dangerous as a special defense, the AMA resolution would allow psychiatric testimony to be considered during trials if it showed that the defendants did not know what they were doing, and thus did not have the intent to commit crimes. The AMA resolution would also allow psychiatric testimony to be introduced at the times of sentencing so that judges could better decide the fate of defendants.

As we'll now see in the final chapter, a number of changes in the plea are currently being proposed for enactment into law by the U.S. Congress, and a number have already been made by the states. If challenged, they may be the developments that at last give us the answer.

7

Action Steps

In this chapter, we'll look at the efforts being made to abolish the insanity plea or alter it significantly, at both the state and federal levels. Then we'll conclude with a report of what one state, Oregon—without altering the plea—is doing to improve its system of handling mentally ill people in trouble with the law.

FEDERAL ACTION

In 1982, President Reagan sent to Congress a body of legislation for consideration and enactment into law. It concerned varied criminal matters and is popularly known as "the President's crime package." It contains a proposal on the insanity plea, with Mr. Reagan recommending that the burden of proof in all insanity trials held under federal law be placed with the defense. If enacted into law, the measure would change the ground rules in all federal courts and would likely encourage the many states that still place the burden with the prosecution to follow suit and adjust their laws accordingly. And, as mentioned in Chapter Six, if enacted, its legality will most likely be challenged.

Over the months following Hinckley's attempted assassination of Mr. Reagan, more than a dozen national political leaders—both senators and representatives—introduced anti-plea bills for congressional study and enactment. They attacked the plea on all fronts.

For instance, in May of 1982, Representative John T. Myers (Republican, Indiana) proposed a bill that would eliminate the plea altogether in federal court. The bill stated simply that "mental condition shall not be a defense to any charge of criminal conduct." The degree of illness, however, would be considered at the time of sentencing, with a decision being made as to psychiatric care for the convicted defendant.

Four other bills—authored separately by Senator Edward Zorinsky (Democrat, Nebraska) and Representatives F. James Sensenbrenner, Jr. (Republican, Wisconsin), Howard S. Sawyer (Democrat, Michigan), and Matthew J. Rinaldo (Republican, New Jersey)—all called for the use of the guilty-but-mentally-ill verdict in federal law. The wording of Representative Sensenbrenner's bill reflected what the several proposals had to say. The Sensenbrenner bill would authorize defendants to be found guilty but mentally ill if their actions constituted all the necessary elements of the charged offense other than the requisite state of mind (did not know what they were doing) and if that requisite state of mind was the result of a mental disease or defect.

The bills all authorize punishment for defendants found guilty but mentally ill. The defendants would, of course, be entitled to psychiatric treatment and after recovery would be made to serve the remainder of their sentences.

A similar bill came from Republican Senator Orrin Hatch of Utah. He, too, proposed that defendants be judged solely on the basis of whether they had the requisite state of mind for the charged offense. His bill holds that they could be found not guilty on the grounds of insanity only if it is proved that they did not know what they were doing. Confinement for care would follow, with a court then to release a defendant only if the preponderance of evidence at the time indicated that the defendant was no longer a danger to self or society.

At the time this book is being written, no final action has been taken on either President Reagan's "crime package" or the various bills. All remain under congressional study, with final rejection or enactment to come at some future time.

Remember, however, that any of the bills, if passed, will very likely face a series of court challenges as to their legality under the Constitution.

STATE ACTION

Although action at the federal level is still pending, many states have already taken definite steps against the plea.

Both Montana and Idaho—Montana in 1979 and Idaho in 1982—have barred the use of the insanity plea. Both, however, require their courts to hold hearings on the mental health of defendants. The hearings are held at the time of sentencing and are intended to determine the psychiatric care that will be needed while the prison term is being served.

At the time Hinckley went to court, five states had laws permitting the use of the guilty-but-mentally-ill verdict. They were Georgia, Illinois, Indiana, Michigan, and New Jersey. Since then, the list has grown to eight with the addition of Alaska, Delaware, and Kentucky. Other states are presently considering similar legislation.

California has taken an interesting step to tighten its control over the use of the insanity plea. In a ballot measure voted into law in 1982, the state returned to the basic points in the M'Naghton Rule. However, it altered a single word in the rule, a one-word revision that made the rule far more difficult on defendants. See if you can find the change in the following:

Section 25 of California's penal law now reads that, in any criminal proceeding (including that for juveniles) in which a plea of not guilty by reason of insanity is attempted, the verdict will be in favor of the defendant "only when the accused person proves by a preponderance of the evidence that he or she was incapable (1) of knowing or understanding the nature or the quality of his or her act and (2) of distinguishing right from wrong at the time the act was committed."

The change, of course, is that California law uses the word *and* rather than M'Naghton's *or* between the two points. No longer are attorneys able to defend clients on the basis of one point or the other. *Both* points must be established before a not-guilty verdict is possible.

California has also moved against the plea of diminished capacity, the plea that can have a defendant found only partially guilty because of insanity and thus charged with a lesser crime and given a lighter sentence. The state's penal law—again, in Section 25—now reads that "the defense of diminished capacity is hereby abolished." The code then goes on: "In a criminal action, as well as any juvenile court proceeding, evidence concerning an accused person's intoxication, trauma, mental illness, disease, or defect shall not be admissible" in court if it is for the purpose of showing that the defendant was incapable, through diminished capacity, of forming the motive, the intent, or the malice aforethought necessary to make the offense a crime.

In great part, California has moved against the diminished capacity defense because of public anger over the outcome of the Dan White case. That case, you'll recall, was explained in Chapter Three.

THE OREGON SYSTEM

In 1978, to facilitate the handling of insanity cases, the state of Oregon instituted a program found nowhere else in the nation. It formed a group known as the Psychiatric Security Review Board. Placed with the board was the responsibility of supervising the futures of all defendants acquitted on the grounds of insanity.

The board operates independently of the Oregon court system and the state's various mental hospitals, thus relieving both the courts and the hospitals from the time-consuming legal and medical questions involved when considering whether patients should be released from confinement for care.

All mentally ill persons acquitted of a crime are placed under the board's jurisdiction for the maximum length of time they would have served in prison had they been found guilty of their charged offenses. At virtually any time during that period, they may petition the board to be released from confinement for care. Depending on their condition, the petition may be granted or rejected. If judged sufficiently well, they can be awarded either an unconditional or conditional release. An unconditional release sees them freed from the board's jurisdiction and entitled to live their own lives. A conditional release calls for them to be cared for on an out-patient basis and continues to hold them under the board's supervision. That supervision can be maintained for years after they have left the hospital— for as long as the board deems it necessary.

All persons acquitted, however, are released from the board's control once they've reached the maximum time they would have served in prison. Should any patient still be so dangerous at that time as to require further confinement, other laws in the state make it possible for the confinement to continue.

Oregon law sets the board's membership at five. The present membership is made up of men and women from different walks of life, but each with an interest in the work and most with a professional expertise in it. Serving at the time this book is being written are a private citizen, an attorney, a psychiatrist, a psychologist, and a parole officer. Assisting them is a three-member professional staff. Some 300 persons are currently under the board's jurisdiction.

To see how the board works, let's say that you're a patient seeking release from confinement for care. You would appear before the board with your attorney and the two of you would answer questions and speak on your behalf. (If you could not afford an attorney, the board would appoint one to represent you, at no cost to you.) The hospital staff would give their recommendations. Your records would be examined. Then, in private, the board would consider all aspects of your request and return to tell you the decision. Throughout the proceedings, because you are the one bringing the request, you would carry the burden of proving that you are, indeed, fit for either conditional or unconditional release. Right at the start, the board would inform you that it's your responsibility to establish that proof by "a preponderance of the evidence."

Were you to be granted a conditional release, you would almost certainly be assigned to care on an outpatient basis. You would have to report regularly, perhaps even daily, to a hospital or a mental health facility for treatment. At the same time, a health worker would call on you periodically to help in your return to normal living and to make sure that your condition remains stable. Should you be on a psychotropic medication, you'd be closely watched to see that you don't stop taking it. At least once a month, the people caring for you would report your progress to the board.

Now let's say that for some reason—perhaps for forgetting to take your medication—your condition reverses itself and you threaten to become a danger again to yourself or society. The board will be immediately informed. It can then quickly issue a warrant for your confinement. Within hours you can be returned to the hospital.

In all, it is the board's duty to supervise you as you attempt a recovery and, at the same time, to protect the Oregon public against your possible return to behavior patterns that could result in further violent offenses. The public protection demanded of the board is seen in its very name—the Psychiatric Security Review Board.

In its 1983 television program on insanity and the law, NBC reported on the work of the board, with commentator Edwin Newman saying that the Oregon system might well be one that could be used as a model to be followed nationally. The American Psychiatric Association recently issued a report voicing substantially the same opinion.

That, indeed, the Oregon system might become a national model seems a good possibility. In the wake of the NBC telecast, the office of the board reports that it has received queries from several states on the board's work, all with an eye to considering the establishment of similar systems there. Among the states seeking information have been New Mexico and New Jersey. Should the system be adopted on a national scale and should it prove successful, it could mark a major solution to the many problems surrounding the insanity plea.

At this point, we come to the close of the book. We've looked at all aspects of the insanity plea and the national debate raging over it. We've discussed the plea itself, the arguments for and against abandoning it, the arguments for and against changing it in any way, and the steps that are being proposed or being taken to solve its many problems.

In light of all that we've talked about, only one question remains: Where do you stand in the debate and what do you think should be done about the plea?

Recommended Reading List

If you would like to read more about the insanity plea, you will find the following books and magazine articles especially helpful.

BOOKS

Coughlin, George Gordon. *Law for the Layman.* New York: Harper & Row, 1975

Hanna, John Paul. *The Complete Layman's Guide to the Law.* Englewood, New Jersey: Prentice-Hall, 1974

Lubin, Martin. *Good Guys, Bad Guys.* New York: McGraw-Hill, 1982

Park, Clara Clairborne, with Shapiro, Leon N. *You Are Not Alone.* Boston: Little, Brown, 1976

Sifakis, Carl. *The Encyclopedia of American Crime.* New York: Facts on File, Inc., 1982

Winslade, William J. and Ross, Judith Wilson. *The Insanity Plea.* New York: Scribner's, 1983

MAGAZINE ARTICLES

Buckley, William F. "The Hinckley Mess." *National Review*, July 23, 1982

Cohen, Stephen. "It's a Mad, Mad Verdict." *The New Republic*, July 12, 1982

Ennis, Bruce J. "Straight Talk About the Insanity Defense." *The Nation*, July 24-31, 1982

Hatch, Orrin. "The Insanity Defense Is Insane." *Reader's Digest*, October, 1982

Hinckley, Jack and Jo Ann. "Illness Is the Culprit." *Reader's Digest*, March, 1983

Hinckley, John. "The Insanity Defense and Me." *Newsweek*, September 20, 1981

Johnson, Brian D. "The Trials of the Insanity Plea." *Maclean's*, July 5, 1982

Kaufman, Irving R. "The Insanity Plea on Trial." *New York Times Magazine*, August 8, 1982

McMillan, Priscilla Johnson. "An Assassin's Portrait." *The New Republic*, July 12, 1982

Stone, Marvin. "Hinckley's Insanity Plea." *U.S. News & World Report*, May 17, 1982

U.S. News & World Report. "The Insanity Plea Is on Trial Again." May 10, 1982

_____"Hinckley Bombshell: End of Insanity Pleas?" July 5, 1982

Index

Parr, Jerry, 4, 7, 8
Partial insanity. *See* Diminished
  capacity
Peel, Sir Robert, 25
Petitions for release, 17, 38–39,
  41, 45, 48, 70–71, 83, 94–95
Precedents, 24, 26, 28
Premeditation, 33–35
Preponderance of the evidence,
  37, 85, 92, 95
Pressler, Larry, 57–59, 73
Prison, 17, 41, 71, 78–81, 91–92
Proof, burden of. *See* Burden
Protection, public, 62–64, 78, 87
Psychiatric care:
  and guilty-but-insane verdict,
    78
  under Oregon system, 94–96
  outpatient, 38, 42, 45–48, 64,
    71
  and pending legislation, 91–
    92
  in prison, 41, 71, 78
Psychiatric Security Review Board
  (Oregon), 94–96
Psychiatric testimony, 51–59, 67–
  69
  paid. *see* Witnesses, profes-
    sional
  proposed restrictions on, 81–
    83
  slanted, 54–57, 67–69, 82, 84
  and wealth, 57–59, 73–74
Public opinion surveys, 43–44
Public pressure to convict, 66
Punishment *vs.* rehabilitation, 62–
  65, 79–81

Ray, James Earl, 7
Reader's Digest, 46, 49, 99
Reagan, Ronald, 3–8, 18, 90–91,
  93
Reasonable doubt, 36, 84
Rehabilitation, 62–65, 79–81
  see also Psychiatric care
Release:
  under Oregon system, 94–96
  public fear of, 17–18, 41–44,
    66

unwise, 43–48, 69–73, 87
  see also Petitions for release
Requisite state of mind, 13–14,
  88, 91–92
Revenge motive, 12, 28, 31, 35
Revenge, public, 61–62, 64–66, 79
"Rich man's defense," 57–59, 73–
  74
Right and wrong, knowledge of,
  24, 30
Rinaldo, Matthew J., 91
Roosevelt, Theodore, 39–41

St. Elizabeth's Hospital, 16–17, 44,
  51
Sawyer, Howard S., 91
Schrank, John, 39–41
Self-defense, 12, 28, 31
Sensenbrenner, F. James, Jr., 91
Sirhan, Sirhan B., 7, 11
Special defense status, 37–38, 86–
  87
State action against plea, 92–94
Supreme Court (U.S.) decisions,
  85–86

Taxi Driver, 9–11
Time of act, insanity at, 32
Tradition, basis in, 16, 21 ff., 32,
  62
Trapnell, Garrett, *50*, 51, 69, 70
Trial procedure, 36–38

Valium, 49, 53
Verdict:
  guilty but mentally unbal-
    anced, 77–81, 91, 92
  restrictions on, 76

Wallace, George, 7
Wealth as legal factor, 57–59, 73–
  74
White, Dan, *34*, 35–36, 94
Witnesses, professional, 54–56,
  68–69
  court-appointed, 83–84
  state-employed, 69–83

Zorinsky, Edward, 91